SETTING STRATEGIC GOALS AND OBJECTIVES

THE WEST SERIES IN STRATEGIC MANAGEMENT

Consulting Editor
Charles W. Hofer

Setting Strategic Goals and Objectives, 2d ed.
Max D. Richards

Strategy Formulation: Issues and Concepts
Charles W. Hofer

Strategy Formulation: Power and Politics, 2d ed.
Ian C. MacMillan and Patricia E. Jones

Strategy Implementation: Structure, Systems, and Process, 2d ed.
Jay R. Galbraith and Robert K. Kazanjian

Strategic Control
Peter Lorange, Michael F. Scott Morton, and Sumantra Ghoshal

Macroenvironmental Analysis for Strategic Management
Liam Fahey and V. K. Narayanan

Second Edition

SETTING STRATEGIC GOALS AND OBJECTIVES

Max D. Richards

CRUMMER GRADUATE SCHOOL OF BUSINESS
ROLLINS COLLEGE

WEST PUBLISHING COMPANY

St. Paul New York Los Angeles San Francisco

Copyediting by Joan Torkildson

Interior art by Alice B. Thiede, Carto-Graphics

Cover design by Peter Thiel, Kim Rafferty

Typesetting by Huron Valley Graphics, Inc. Typefaces are Aster and Optima.

50 West Kellogg Boulevard
P.O. Box 64526
St. Paul, MN 55164-1003

Printed in the United States of America

Library of Congress Cataloging-in-Publication Data

Richards, Max De Voe, 1923–
Setting strategic goals and objectives.

(The West series in strategic management)
Bibliography: p.
Includes index.
1. Management by objectives. I. Title.
HD30.65.R53 1986 658.4'012 85-22447
ISBN 0-314-85291-3

CONTENTS

FOREWORD

This series is a response to the rapid and significant changes that have occurred in the strategic management/business policy area over the past twenty-five years. Although strategic management/business policy is a subject of long standing in management schools, it was traditionally viewed as a capstone course whose primary purpose was to *integrate* the knowledge and skills students had gained in the functional disciplines. During the past fifteen years, however, strategic management/business policy has developed a substantive content of its own. Originally, this content focused on the concepts of corporate and business strategies and on the processes by which such strategies were formulated and implemented within organizations. More recently, as Figure 1 and Table 1 illustrate, the scope of the field has broadened to include the study of both the functions and responsibilities of top management and the organizational systems and processes used to establish overall organizational goals and objectives and to formulate, implement, and control the strategies and policies necessary to achieve these goals and objectives.

When the *West Series in Business Policy and Planning* was originally published, most of the texts in the field did not yet reflect this extension in scope. The principal purpose of the original series was, therefore, to fill this void by incorporating the latest research findings and conceptual thought in the field into each of the texts in the series. In the intervening seven years, the series has succeeded to a far greater degree than we could have ever hoped.

However, the pace of research in strategic management/business policy has, if anything, increased since the publication of the original series. Some changes are, thus, clearly in order. It is the purpose of the *West Series in Strategic Management* to continue the tradition

Figure 1 The Evolution of Business Policy/Strategic Management as a Field of Study

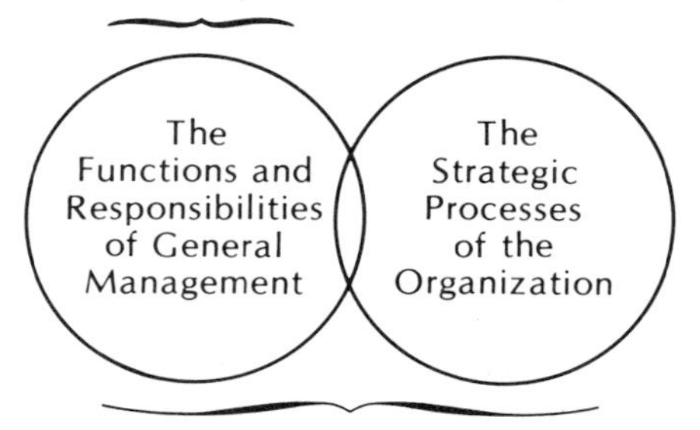

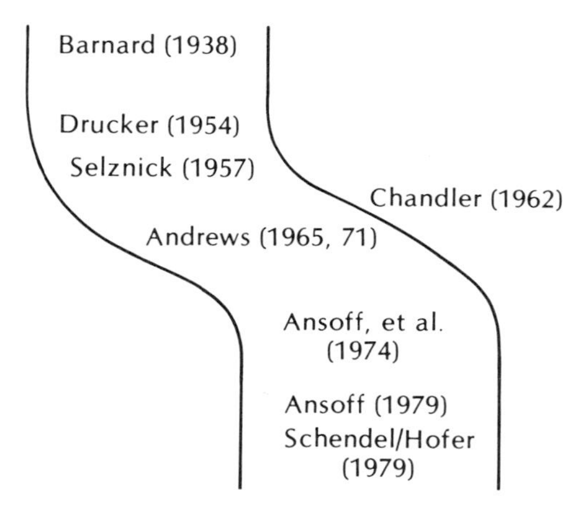

of innovative, state-of-the-art coverage of the field of strategic management started by the *West Series in Business Policy and Planning* both through revisions to all the books in the original series and through the addition of two new titles. In making such revisions, care has been taken to ensure not only that the various texts fit together as a series, but also that each is self-contained and addresses a major topic in the field. In addition, the series has been designed so that it covers almost all the major topics that form the

Table 1 The Major Subfields of Business Policy/Strategic Management

	1. Boards of Directors
	2. The Nature of General Management Work
	3. Middle-Level General Management
*	4. Stakeholder Analysis
✓	5. Organizational Goal Formulation
*	6. Corporate Social Policy and Management Ethics
	7. Macroenvironmental Analysis
*	8. Strategy Formulation and Strategic Decision Making
	9. Corporate-Level Strategy (including Mergers, Acquisitions, and Divestitures)
	10. Business-Level Strategy
	11. Strategic Planning and Information Systems
*	12. The Strategy-Structure-Performance Linkage
	13. The Design of Macroorganizational Structure and Systems
	14. Strategic Control Systems
	15. Organizational Culture
	16. Leadership Style for General Managers
	17. The Strategic Management of Small Businesses and New Ventures
	18. The Strategic Management of High Tech Organizations
	19. The Strategic Management of Not-for-Profit Organizations

✓ Indicates subfields that are covered extensively by this text
* Indicates other subfields that are discussed in this text

heartland of strategic management, as Figure 2 illustrates. The individual texts in the series are

Setting Strategic Goals and Objectives, 2d ed.
Max D. Richards

Strategy Formulation: Issues and Concepts
Charles W. Hofer

Strategy Formulation: Power and Politics, 2d ed.
Ian C. MacMillan and Patricia E. Jones

Strategy Implementation: Structure, Systems, and Process, 2d ed.
Jay R. Galbraith and Robert K. Kazanjian

Strategic Control
Peter Lorange, Michael F. Scott Morton, and Sumantra Ghoshal

Macroenvironmental Analysis for Strategic Management
Liam Fahey and V. K. Narayanan

Figure 2 The Strategic Management Process

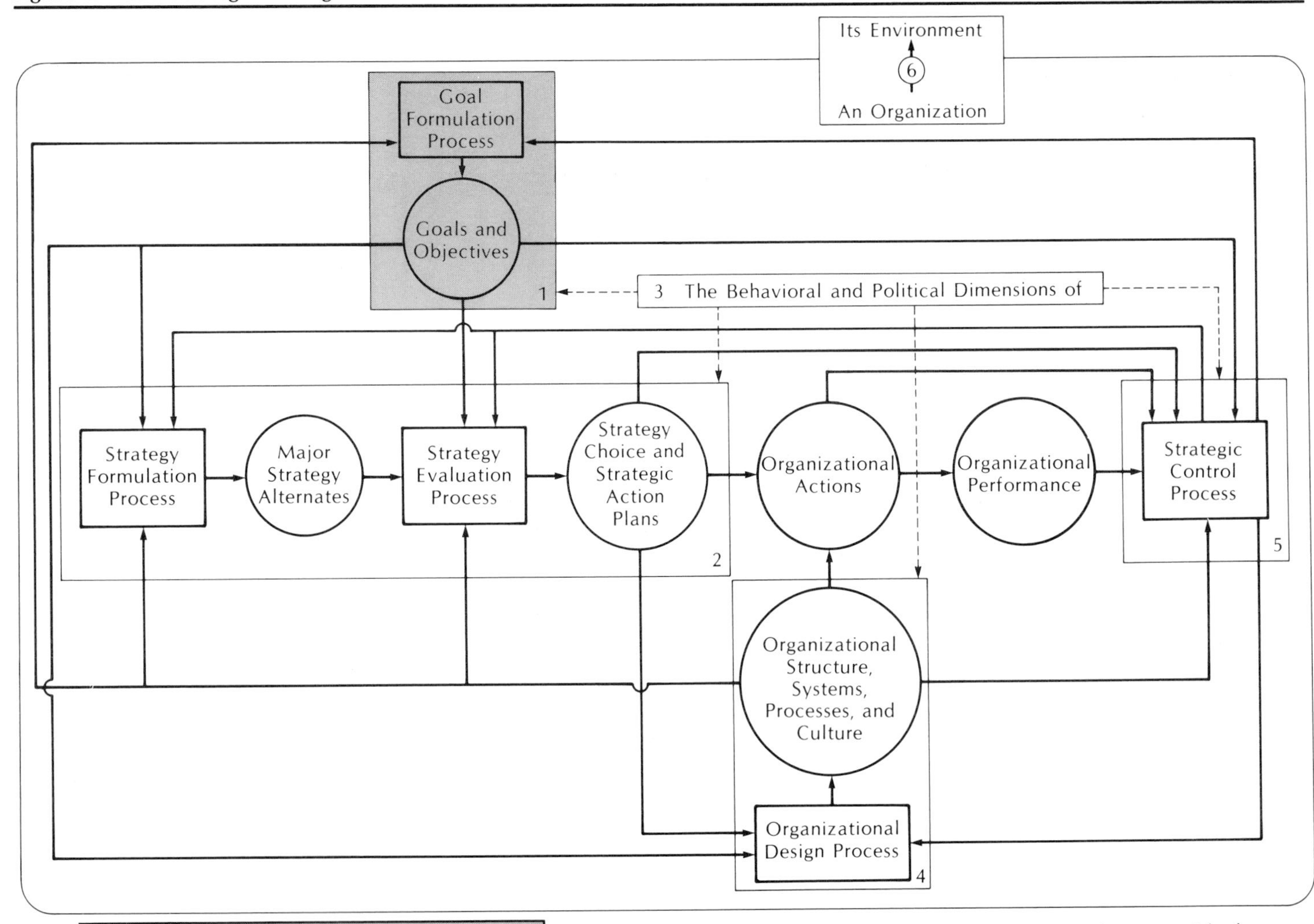

The series has also been designed so that the texts within it can be used in several ways. First, the entire series can be used as a set to provide an advanced conceptual overview of the field of strategic management. Second, selected texts in the series can be combined with cases drawn from the Harvard Case Services, the Case Teaching Association, and/or the Case Research Association to create a course customized to particular instructor needs. Third, individual texts in the series can be used to supplement the conceptual materials contained in the existing text and casebooks in the field. The series thus offers the individual instructor great flexibility in designing the required business policy/strategic management course. Fourth, because of their self-contained nature, each of the texts can be used either individually or in combination with other materials as the basis for an advanced specialized course in strategic management. For instance, the text on *Strategic Control* could be used to create a state-of-the-art course on the "Strategic Control Systems." Likewise, the *Macroenvironmental Analysis for Strategic Management* and *Strategy Formulation: Power and Politics* texts could be combined to create an innovative course on "Stakeholder Management." Or the text on *Setting Strategic Goals and Objectives* could be combined with a text on boards of directors to create an advanced course on the latter topic.

Finally, in concluding this Common Foreword I would like to thank my co-editor on the original series, Dan Schendel of Purdue University, for his efforts on that series. They were both substantial and valuable. Indeed, the series could not have been established as effectively as it was without him.

Charles W. Hofer
Editor
October 1985

PREFACE

An explicit examination of the nature and development of goals is frequently not undertaken. Too often, goals are assumed. Profit is the expected goal of business firms. A hospital, or other organization, may not articulate specific goals because, if it does, it may have to meet them. Managers who wish to maximize the achievement of their organizations, however, must pay attention to what is sought and the expected level of achievement—in other words, to strategic goals and objectives, the subject of this book.

Although few comprehensive treatments of goals or objectives exist, bits and pieces may be found in a number of areas: economic and management science literature, behavioral and political sources, strategy-policy writings, social responsibility literature, and concepts from the management by objectives approach to managing. A major purpose of this book is to enable managers from any organization to integrate materials or goals and objectives from these diverse sources.

We should recognize, however, that goals and objectives that represent overall purposes of an organization merely describe where the organization wants to go rather than how to get there. As we shall see in this book, the where and the how are intricately related. The content, level, and timing of an objective effectively limit the range of alternatives that can best be employed in reaching that goal. Conversely, selection of a particular strategy for an organization may effectively limit the subset of objectives toward which it can reasonably strive. Accordingly, the interrelationship between objectives and other planning and operations within the enterprise is a topic that receives attention throughout the book.

The new title of this edition, *Setting Strategic Goals and Objectives,* emphasizes the action-oriented process of setting goals. The title further differentiates between goals (defined here as the general statement of purpose) and objectives (specific as to measure, level, content, and timing). A new chapter on establishing economic objectives deals with some practical approaches to the goal-setting process and, at the same time, considers the conflicting factors that bear upon the decisions of what the economic objectives of a firm should be. Clarification of old material and the addition of new material have produced substantial revisions in some parts of the book.

Any attempt to present a comprehensive overview of a complex topic is indebted to many previous writers, researchers, and practitioners as well as to experts of corollary materials. In the West Series in Strategic Management, the efforts of the other authors provide materials with which to interact. The original design of the series is thus responsible for creating a relationship among the several books in the series. We can better understand policy and strategy by looking at them from a number of perspectives. This book offers the perspectives of establishing objectives at the strategic and substrategic levels, integrating the objectives at several levels within and outside the enterprise, and coordinating the goals with strategic planning and accomplishment.

Few of you will recall that I acknowledged Ruth Nixon in the first edition. She has since become my wife and was once again of great assistance. Martin Schatz, Dean of the Crummer Graduate School of Business, was most gracious and encouraging in providing support during the writing and typing of this edition. I have benefited as well from the advice of many people including Charles Hofer, University of Georgia; Anthony M. Akel, Long Island University; and Kurt Christiansen, Northwestern University. Thus the book represents the integration of materials from many sources at one point in time. Nonetheless, the result is, of course, my responsibility alone.

Max D. Richards
Winter Park, Florida
July 1985

SETTING STRATEGIC GOALS AND OBJECTIVES

1

Underlying Factors in Setting Goals and Objectives

This chapter undertakes to explain the rationale in setting strategic goals and corporate objectives. To do this, we examine the nature of goals and objectives and the purposes they serve, particularly in the context of organizations. We differentiate goals from objectives: Goals are general and open-ended statements of purpose, whereas objectives are specific, closed-end statements. We conclude by examining how one can develop a better set of goals or objectives or both.

WHY WORRY ABOUT GOALS?

The objectives of an organization inform us about *what* is to be accomplished. Strategy tells us *how*. Both need to be considered equally. This book serves individuals seeking to establish goals and objectives for their organizations. It also serves those individuals who wish to know more about organizations through a better understanding of goal-setting processes and the effects of goal-directed activity upon managers and clients of organizations.

Christensen et al. (1982, 20) claim that "The most difficult role . . . of the chief executive of any organization is the one in which he serves as custodian of corporate objectives." This role is difficult because it is complex and requires utmost care. If the underlying purposes of an organization are unclear or not well communicated, coordination of efforts and the rationale of the organization are lost. Carefully considered objectives help avoid misdirection, vacillation, and mere drifting. Thus there is an urgent priority to setting appropriate goals. Goals provide destinations and greater certainty for decisions rather than continual improvisation in where to go.

Equally important, properly set goals provide company character and identity and help establish the role the organization will play in society. Corporate purpose leads the behaviors of managers and workers in their respective roles within the organization. Goals, objectives, and purposes provide the ends toward which action should be directed.

PURPOSES SERVED BY GOALS

Setting a corporate purpose that members of the organization can identify with and be proud of is an ennobling act. To be "number one" or "the best manufacturing company in the world" are goals worthy of sustained efforts. Wise leaders know that properly established objectives allow participants to willingly subjugate their personal goals to the common good.

> Penn State football coach Joe Paterno, in his quest to have a top-ranked team, set forth his philosophies for his scholar-athlete "grand experiment" in *Football My Way*. His ideas were attractive to players, fans, and observers far and wide. A Penn State professor was sharply reminded of this while stepping off a plane in Malaysia, when his Asian host asked, "Do you know Joe Paterno?"

Conversely, while goals such as "maximizing shareholders' returns" may be worthy and even lofty, they may fail to gain the feeling of identity and élan from some participants in the organization (labor members in this instance). The search for an ennobling purpose is thus an important priority of the leadership of any organization.

A goal provides *guidance* to the direction of efforts of individuals in organizations. Having both beauty and functionality as goals in the design of a skyscraper will lead the architect in directions different from an objective of "minimizing costs per square foot of rentable space."

Similarly, goals affect the *planning* that the organization undertakes. A firm attempting to grow at a rapid rate and to increase its market share will require a planning effort that carefully examines the particular customers, their uses of the products involved, the potential for more sales to those customers, the same sort of analysis for unsold customers, the probable attractiveness of the firm's products to customers, and so on. Efforts to achieve high levels of new product introduction would be probable. More extensive and intensive planning would be required to achieve the growth goal than if the objective were stability and maintenance of market share.

The use of objectives can provide *motivation* and inspiration to individuals in the organization to perform at higher levels of efficiency and effectiveness. Closed objectives establish the level of expectations for performance. Individuals can establish their own goals and be motivated by them. Students establishing and committing themselves to an A average, for example, provide self-motivation and inspiration to their efforts. Managers, too, can establish personal goals. Yet, it is to the organizational goals that subordinate behavior must also be directed and motivated. To ensure motivation, the manager needs to examine through ends-means-ends analysis the logic of what is expected for subordinates to achieve.

Objectives may form the basis for *evaluating* and *controlling* activity. The United Fund campaign in a moderate-sized city might establish a goal of contributions from individuals as five dollars per capita. Such a goal would engender plans by the subchairman in charge of contacting individuals for solicitation, approaches to solicitation, and efforts of volunteers to obtain contributions and pledges. If, during the campaign, a contribution level of only four dollars per capita was being achieved, control efforts to determine why the variance occurred, whether it was due to the plans, the levels of goal established in the first place, or other reasons could be examined for revision of subsequent behaviors.

Thus, goals and objectives permeate the whole management process, providing an underpinning for planning efforts, direction, motivation, and control. In organizations, managers are involved in these activities on a continual basis. Without goals and communication of them, behaviors in managerial processes can meander in any direction.

FAILURE IN ACHIEVING GOALS

In classic economics, maximization of profits is the assumed goal of a business firm. Managers are "rational" insofar as their decisions have that maximizing effect. Deviation from maximization results in suboptimization. Suboptimization results in costs that can be measured, theoretically, by the difference between what occurred and what would have resulted from the optimum solution. In the classic economic model, suboptimization stems from irrational choices, since a correct decision from a rational manager would have resulted in the maximization of goal achievement. Thus, from the point of view of the firm, rationality is linked to optimization, and irrationality is linked to suboptimization. Similarly, rational optimizing behavior is "good" for society, because resources were used most efficiently in creating value. Conversely, irrationality and suboptimization are "bad," because resources are wasted.

Sources of Suboptimization

In most organizations employing multiple objectives, the chances for suboptimization multiply greatly beyond those organizations devoted to a single goal. First, the objectives themselves may be in conflict, so that achievement of one is at the expense of one or more other goals. Line B in Figure 1.1 exemplifies the posited relationships when achievement of Y results in lesser performance on the X goal. Some inventors who start businesses to exploit one of their creations have become highly successful in the market. When this occurs, the business requires additional plant, equipment, and working capital to produce and sell the expanding product volume. Yet, the business ordinarily will not create the profits and cash flows to finance the investments required from rapid growth. Thus, the firm is forced to enter the financial markets to obtain resources to support its success. If entrepreneurs also wish to retain ownership control so that they may reap the benefits of their own creativity, they want to avoid selling equity to outsiders. For some time, the firm can borrow until the growth requires a level of debt unacceptable to the lenders. At that time, slowing growth or giving up majority equity control are

Figure 1.1 Types of Complementarity Relations Among Goals

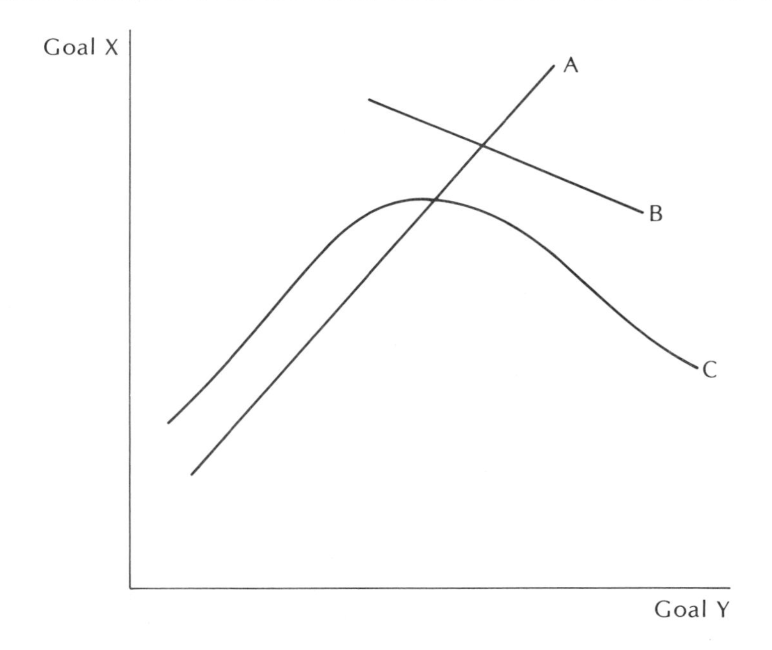

the primary alternatives remaining to entrepreneurs. Slow growth, however, invites competitors to enter and, if continued, could result in a loss of market share such that competitors would dominate the market. Such a market share scenario is also unacceptable to entrepreneurs who seek to reap the benefits of their creation. High growth resulting from product success, retaining majority equity control, and reaping the benefits of the creative effort are inconsistent goals for many highly successful small firms.

The inconsistency among goals is just as prevalent in large firms. Hatten and Schendel (1976) show that attempts to achieve higher market share by large national breweries has been at the expense of their profitability. Schoeffler, Buzzell, and Heany (1974) echo this observation and show that attempts to increase product quality or research and development are associated with declining profits. High share or quality or R&D are associated with high profits, but changes in them are inversely related to profitability. The implications of their research for the strategic choice of goal levels of these firms is to maintain rather than increase market share, if such a goal is not to be inconsistent with achieving a profit goal. If these firms consider market share to be more important than profits, profits may be thought of as a constraint (which cannot be negative for long periods).

A set of goals may be complementary, as is shown in line A of Figure 1.1. Improving managerial capabilities through executive development, for example, may be positively related to profitability. More likely, the relation resembles that of curve C, which indicates complementarity among goals at some levels of expenditure and inconsistency at other levels.

Although inconsistency among corporate objectives brings about suboptimization, the problem also arises because the goals of subparts of a system may interact in such a way as to have a deleterious impact upon overall goals. If the production department schedules long runs of parts to minimize its labor costs (a reasonable production goal among several), larger inventories of parts will be required. In turn, more inventory investment increases the investment base against which overall corporate profit is measured. Thus, by minimizing labor costs, return on investment could be adversely affected. If lowering labor costs does not result in increased profits sufficient to offset the rise in inventory investment, suboptimization with respect to the return on investment objective occurs.

The problem is analogous to attempting to apply optimizing management science models to a totality of operations of an organization. The problem is so large and complex that no computer model has been successful in dealing with it. Consequently, a separation of the overall into subproblems, and the solution for each, is made. When the subproblem solutions are added, however, their separate optimization fails to result in overall optimization of the decision.

Satisficing Versus Optimizing

In spite of the best available technology of management, then, suboptimization occurs. This results from the large scale of complexity in modern organizations. The sheer number of factors affecting an important decision places substantial information, modeling, and computational requirements upon the decision maker. Furthermore, there are often considerable time pressures on managers to arrive at a decision quickly. There is then insufficient time to gather the required data even if it were available. As a consequence, managers must and do act on less than full information. Rather than seeking all alternatives, they search until there is a satisfactory solution, frequently selecting the first available solution that meets their goals. If no satisfactory alternative is found, either additional search is undertaken or, ultimately, the objectives used are lowered so that one of the alternatives available fits within the revised criteria. If a salesperson needs a new car for her job, and her search is unable to find one that meets all of her preestablished criteria, she may buy one without one of her requirements—for example, a differential traction transmission. She has not optimized, but the value of additional search, given her immediate need for a car, is not worth the effort.

The above process is suboptimizing and irrational in the classic economic sense. Yet, it may be good management if time requirements and information costs are considered. March and Simon (1958) have labeled such a decision process as *satisficing* to distinguish it from maximizing behavior. Many scholars are uncomfortable with the satisficing concept, because they associate it with the bad connotations held about suboptimization. The classic economic model assumptions of complete knowledge, unlimited computational capacities, and knowledge of the probabilities of future events are unrealistic in large complex modern organizations. Satisficing decisions may be all that can be expected.

Organizational Versus Personal Goals

This book focuses upon goals of organizations. Although some authors contend that only people have goals and organizations reflect purposes sought by a collection of people, clearly organizations cannot satisfy all the goals of all its members. Many of us seek better health as a goal, yet until recently, few enterprises, other than health care organizations, directly serviced this personal goal. Today, a number of firms believe that personal health of employees and goals of the firm are complementary. These organizations provide resources, advice, and encouragement for improving employee health. Many of us are also interested in greater personal affluence. If the organizations for which we work were to attempt to maximize all of our desires for personal affluence, they would soon become bankrupt.

Yet, organizations cannot ignore individual goals in their operation. They do provide rewards to individuals who can use the receipts to satisfy their personal needs. Indeed, some organizational activity can directly serve the goals of some individuals. A personal goal to achieve power and influence in the community may be possible by working for a political or governmental agency. Individuals starting their own business to meet a personal objective of employing their relatives can, if successful, exert enough power to achieve personal goals through the organization.

So far as personal goals are different from organizational goals, individuals pursuing their own ends create suboptimization. Yet, we attempt to find complementarity between organizational and personal objectives.

Retreat from Objectives

In his interesting analysis of objectives for federal social programs, Wildavsky (1979) shows that the difficulty (even impossibility) of achieving goals results in behaviors that attempt to show organizational success while failing to meet the intended goal. For example, decentralization of the model cities program to the states allowed the federal government to shift their failure to solve housing problems to local communities. The latter were unable to make the trade-offs any better.

Rather than reduce crime, we attempt to decriminalize gambling, prostitution, and marijuana usage or to start early parole procedures. We deinstitutionalize the mentally ill, expecting relatively unprepared local communities to solve the problem. We provide equal access to health care rather than making people healthier. Rather than educate the hard core, we change students to those who can be retrained.

Wildavsky attributes failure to achieve objectives in social programs to the difficulty of changing personal behaviors. Failing to do so, agencies resort to decentralization, deinstitutionalization, deeducation, decriminalization, and demedicalizing—his five Ds. While private businesses can focus upon profit and their derivatives, public agencies in charge of social programs cannot. Private firms can terminate employees; public agencies must serve qualified clients even though they cannot change the behaviors important in implementing the program.

Private business firms are only partially insulated from these behaviors. CPAs, for example, certify that the firm's accounts are in conformity with generally accepted accounting principles consistently applied. They do not certify, however, that the accounts truly represent transactions, status of the financial position of the firm, or a host of other things we might like to know (e.g., bribes to foreign officials). The goal of truth is subverted to the objective of "procedures applied consistently." Is truth an impossible goal here?

EFFECTS OF GOAL DIFFERENCES ON BEHAVIOR

Compare the differences in strategies and subgoals between two football teams with different overall goals: winning the Super Bowl versus a rebuilding year. A rebuilding team seeks to develop and give experience to younger players with potential for helping win in later years. In a rebuilding season, the team will sacrifice winning to provide game experience to rookies. It will trade proven veterans near retirement to acquire high-potential draft choices. The emphasis is upon the future.

The team seeking to win the season's grand prize will use its best players. They will be withheld from play to allow lesser players opportunity only if injury, lack of veterans' performance, or a big lead in the game warrants these substitutions. The plans for player acquisition, use of players in the game, attention in practice, and the set of actions constituting the team's strategy vary a great deal from those of a rebuilding team.

The two football teams have goals of substantially different *content*. They can be compared to two business firms: one with a primary objective of maximizing its profits and another seeking to increase its share of the market. Strategies and subgoals would be different for the two business firms, as well.

Even if the objectives of two organizations are similar, the way they are measured influences the supporting strategies and subgoals. A number of different measures or indicators of a goal can be used to transform it into a closed-end objective. Profit measures that are used include dollar amount, return on investment, earnings per share of stock, return on equity, and variations or combinations of these.

Sears Roebuck suffered relatively large declines in sales and profits during the 1974–75 recession. Observers attributed Sears' failure to a strategic drift away from their traditional low to moderate price range. Store managers possessed the autonomy to select merchandise lines and were responsible for profits. To increase margins and thereby profits, store managers had tended to drop the lowest priced and lowest margin items. The effect was to reduce store traffic, particularly during recession periods. Less traffic meant that many potential buyers for high-margin items were not drawn into the store in the first place.

To regain Sears' former position, its top management devised a new strategy consisting of centralization of authority and changes in goals. Store managers were made responsible for (1) sales, (2) profits in the store, and (3) profits in the region of which they were a part. The monetary bonuses of store managers were changed to reflect how well they had achieved these objectives. Since revised compensation is based on sales as well as on profits, store managers are more likely to carry and promote low-priced items. Traffic and exposure to high-margin items are thus seen as more likely. Managers will be less prone to overstock and hoard scarce items if other stores in their region can sell them, since managers' bonuses depend on regional profits.

The following lessons are to be learned from the Sears example.

1. Corporate goals cannot be achieved without a consistent strategy. Organization structure, executive staffing, compensation system, and subgoals were all changed to the end of fitting them more closely with overall goals.
2. Managers attend to goals, particularly if they are paid and promoted to do so. Different goals elicit different behaviors. Even different measures of the same objective (profits in this case) change managers' actions.
3. Multiple goals for suborganizations are more likely to further corporate-level objectives than a single one (profit for the store). At the same time, balancing multiple goals will make the store manager's task more complicated.

The following table compares the different strategic actions that can be taken to increase profits in a firm with alternate measures of profit. Decreasing investments of and by itself will not increase profits *if they are measured by return on equity,* but it will increase return on investment. Conversely, increasing the amount of debt relative to stockholders' equity actually decreases profits, other things remaining the same, if profits are measured by *return on investment.* The same action increases profit if it is measured by *return on equity* and if overall profitability rates exceed interest rates on debt. A word of caution is that other things rarely remain the same. Table 1.1 shows some trade-offs between increased profits and coincident risks. Nonetheless, the point to be emphasized is that different profit measures tend to elicit different strategies, such as the following:

Profit Measure Maximized	Examples of Tendencies in Strategy
1. Earnings per share	1. Acquire firms with a lower price earnings ratio.
2. Return on equity	2. Increase the relative proportion of debt in the financial structure if interest is less than ROI.
3. Return on investment	3. Increase sales and margins. Reduce investment per sales dollar.

When experts at turning around the fortunes of failing organizations are brought to the rescue, they are often faced with managerial and worker groups demoralized by the prior declines in performance, employment, customer complaints, and so on. Turnaround managers claim that it is important to focus on one achievable goal from among many available. While achievable (Banaszewski 1981), the goal must be challenging. When this goal is reached, personnel start to regain their feelings of self-worth and esteem. The interval for achievement allows management to develop a longer-run set of goals that would have been perceived as impossible prior to the achievement of the initial goal, which starts to galvanize the deflated system.

GOALS AND RELATED IDEAS

Goals and objectives have been used interchangeably up to this point. Purpose and ends have provided the same meanings. Closely related to these terms are *guiding philosophies*, which generally constitute statements of the creeds under which the enterprise is expected to operate.

Philosophic creeds may often appear to be platitudinous restatements of "motherhood and country" ideas with which no one disagrees and which are similar from company to company. Illustrating these philosophies are statements that often include beliefs in the free enterprise system, honesty and integrity in dealing with the firm's constituents, and so on. Yet, they can set forth the basic val-

Table 1.1 Increasing Returns and Risks

Actions to Increase Returns	Potential Risks
1. Decrease investment in*	
a. Cash	a. Ability to take cash discounts Decrease in credit worthiness
b. Receivables	b. Loss of credit as marketing tool
c. Fixed capital	c. Outmoded equipment, delivery and scheduling problems, inflexibility of operations
2. Increase sales volume	Overload plant Inventory outages
3. Increase prices selectively	Unit volume reduction Market share loss Experience curve loss
4. Decrease unit costs	Lowered quality
5. Increase debt-to-equity ratio†	Inability to pay interest Lower returns on total investment

* Does not necessarily apply to ROE unless equity is also reduced
† Applies to ROE but not to returns on total investment

ues, aspirations, beliefs, and philosophic priorities under which the firm will operate.

A careful series of statements of values and beliefs can serve the purpose of communicating the special character of the organization to its participants. Lincoln Electric's beliefs that productivity increases shall be shared primarily by employees and customers through higher wages and lower prices (while stockholder's returns are viewed as a constraint) are relatively unique in corporate creeds. These beliefs distinguish Lincoln Electric from other firms and are acted upon by the firm in terms of its specific objectives and operating practices. Thus, its creeds are not trite clichés used as public relations ploys. Rather, they help identify the distinctive corporate self of Lincoln Electric. Well-established philosophic creeds can provide a framework within which goals and (later) strategies may be established.

Other broad, all-encompassing terms include the *corporate mission* and *master strategy*. Both of these terms usually encompass the basic charter, goals, philosophies, and corporate strategy of the firm.

GOAL DEFINITIONS

This book is concerned with an examination of goals and goal processes. Some writers differentiate between goals and objectives, but although one author might define objectives as the means for achieving overall goals, another might reverse this definition. In this book, a goal is defined as a planned position or result to be achieved and is stated in general terms.

Objectives have both a content and a level component. A business firm can have an objective of profitability, or it could alternatively select an objective of achieving the highest quality of products in its industry. The different content of these will, when pursued rationally, result in different behaviors within the organization, since quality is not necessarily consistent with profitability.

Either explicitly or implicitly, each goal also has a *level* component. If the content of the goal is profitability as measured by the return on equity, establishing a return on equity goal of "that consistent with the industry" implies an average return on equity for the firm. This level is different from an alternative level that could be stated, "to achieve the highest return on equity of any firm in our industry." Both the content of the goal and its level influence behaviors within the organization and therefore require careful consideration in their establishment.

Open Versus Closed: Goals or Objectives

Goals may be stated in general terms such as "to achieve better health." This is an open-ended goal, since it is never completely achieved; one presumably could always have better health. A closed objective is achievable and "closed" when met. "To reduce my heartbeat at rest to 55 per minute and my blood pressure to 120/80 in six months" is an example of a closed-end objective. We use *objective* to identify a closed-end goal. Thus we differentiate between goals and objectives by denoting open-ended purposes as goals and closed-end purposes as objectives. In this book, the context of the analysis is also used to determine whether a goal is open or closed.

Open-ended goals are useful in directing activity when great uncertainty prevents immediate specific goal statements to be developed rationally. When a new chief executive takes over a corporation, for example, he may need a period of time to identify the courses of action the firm has the capacity and managers to undertake. During this review period, specific closed-end objectives might well be inadvisable, since they may need to be changed later to reflect the results of the analysis of the firm that the new CEO undertakes.

A second use of open-ended goals is to provide identity, élan (Quinn 1980), and cohesion of effort throughout the organization. At the corporate level, such statements provide the primary thrust toward which the organization is to aim. General Electric's aim to be first or second in every business in which they operate, "All the news that's fit to print" of the *New York Times*, IBM's goal of service, and Lincoln Electric's goal "to be the best manufacturing company in the world" are open-ended goals that establish corporate character. They are close to the guiding philosophy concepts, yet more specific in directing behavior. At the same time, they are not specific enough to prevent discretion in establishing closed-end objectives or a wide range of options to accommodate the open-ended goal.

A third use of open-ended goals is to provide goals at higher levels. General goals are needed at the top levels of an organization, with more specific objectives established at lower organizational levels. The expectation is that the specific objectives at lower levels will be set to achieve the higher-level open-ended goals. An open-ended goal may be met with any number of specific lower-level objectives. If we aim to be "the best manufacturing company in the world," what should be the specific objectives of the research and development department? Should we focus on research to improve manufacturing processes rather than to develop new products? Should we attempt to minimize expenditures to R&D altogether so that more investments in manufacturing equipment can be made? Neither the generality nor the content of the general goal provides guidance on answers to these questions.

Equally unclear is how, during replacement of managers in lower-level departments, the new managers can profitably use specific objectives. If the managers are expected to turn around the operations of a large manufacturing firm, setting initial specific objectives prior to analysis of how to improve and specifically what to aim for after the turnaround could be premature. Thus, open-ended goals for lower-level managers are, at times, also appropriate.

Fourth, an open-ended goal is valuable as an intermediate step in establishing a closed-end objective. A higher-quality product can be operationalized as a closed-end objective by greater specificity as to level and time frame involved.

A mail-order book club sought to reduce errors. Both shipping the wrong book and billing incorrect amounts were identified as quality problems in their service. The objective established was "to decrease shipping and billing errors to 1 percent of orders within one year." To achieve this quality level, order filling and invoicing systems were reorganized, and increased management attention was given to the processes.

Results expected stated as open-ended goals do not allow management to know whether they have ever been achieved. Management can use goals effectively and efficiently if they are stated in closed terms. Later in this chapter, we examine their specificity as a means to make goals more useful.

To arrive at a managerially useful closed-end goal, then, the following are needed.

content	high quality
a measure or indicator	errors made
a level	1 percent of orders
time period	one year

The conditions under which closed-end objectives or open-ended goals tend to be best used are as follows:

Use Open-Ended Goals	Use Closed-End Objectives
During transition or uncertainty	During stability
To provide cohesion, élan, identity	To provide certainty
At higher levels	At lower levels
As a transition to closed-end objectives	To provide specifics to open-ended goals

Ends-Means-Ends Chains

General Electric has a number of ways to achieve its goal of becoming number one or two in each of the businesses in which it participates. For businesses that already meet this goal, a maintenance or improvement strategy may be undertaken. For a business that is a close number three in the market, a market penetration or entry into new markets strategy could be appropriate. Businesses distant from being number one or two may be able to differentiate their product and sell to smaller segments in which they could become number one. All of these strategies can be employed to reach the goal of becoming number one or two.

If a market segmentation and product differentiation strategy is considered, one goal of the marketing department within that business would be to identify market segments and recommend one or more in which the company could achieve its goal. Similarly, the product development people would need to consider how the product or products could be altered to better service the preferred market segments. Production people would need to consider the manufacturing alterations required.

The overall goal triggers a strategy—perhaps new, perhaps reaffirmed. The strategy evokes subgoals, which in turn call for substrategies:

Find Best Combination of Segments and Products		**Market Segmentation and Product Differentiation**		**Number One or Two in Their Business**
Subgoal	⟶	Strategy	⟶	Goal
Ends	⟶	Means	⟶	Ends

The previous example illustrates the differences between strategies and goals. A strategy is a set of actions, policies governing actions, and plans of activity to achieve given results; a goal is a result aspired to. But notice that a strategy also provides additional lower-level goals to be sought by subordinates in the organization.

The subordinate managers would subsequently develop strategies of quality, price, rates of research expenditures, and so on, to support the best service to the product segment subgoal. Thus both process and result can be perceived as an extensive chain of ends-means-ends, linked to each other and the overall goal.

ORGANIZATIONS AS GOAL-SEEKING ENTITIES

Can an organization exist without having a goal? Is there such a thing as an organization that does not pursue at least a survival goal? In examining the behavior of some organizations, observers may find it difficult to identify the particular goal that is being pursued. In discussing goals, however, Krech and Crutchfield (1948, 370) state, "A group does not merely mean individuals characterized by some similar property. Thus, for example, a collection of Republicans or farmers, or Negroes or blind men is not a group." Gibb (1954, 879) states that a functional group "refers to two or more organisms interacting, in the pursuit of a common goal, in such a way that the existence of many is utilized for the satisfaction of some needs of each." Thus, in the view of Gibb, as well as Cyert and March (1963), Simon (1964), and others, an organization would not exist unless it undertook the satisfaction of some common objective. By definition, an organization has a goal or goals.

While organizations are goal seeking, the variation in forming and using objectives is wide. At one extreme are organizations that have established profitability as a single goal whose achievement is relentlessly and diligently pursued. At the opposite end of the spectrum stands an organization whose goals are not stated explicitly, whose statements are unclear to many members of the organization, and whose internal behaviors seem to range so widely that they could be interpreted as contributing to several disparate goals. It may appear that individuals are following lines of activity that maximize their personal values rather than those of the organization. Can such a minimally achieving organization compete and remain viable when opposed in the market by a goal-oriented organization? The rest of this book addresses the explanation of how these differences can occur and their relevance to managers in their use of objectives. Both types of organizations have goals. One has a single objective; the other, many. They represent extremes between which the majority of organizations operate.

MULTIPLE GOALS

Peter Drucker (1954) was one of the early analysts to contend that organizations do and should undertake the achievement of multiple rather than single goals. Economic theory assumes the singularity of profitability as the goal of the business firm in competitive markets. Drucker attacks the notion of emphasizing only profit when he contends that it misdirects managerial effort and encourages the worst practices of management. Specifically, short-run results are favored to the detriment of long-run viability and profitability. Postponable expenses and investments are avoided so that profits and returns during current periods are maximized while jeopardizing longer-term performance. Maintenance expenses can be reduced in a current period at the risk of serious breakdowns later. Research and development to replace maturing products can be delayed to show better current profits.

To balance long- and short-run considerations, Drucker suggests eight key areas in which overall corporate objectives of a business should be established: (1) market standing, (2) innovation, (3) productivity, (4) physical and financial resources, (5) profitability, (6) manager performance and development, (7) worker performance and attitude, and (8) public responsibility. If any of these areas are neglected, it results in subsequent unfavorable consequences. To illustrate, consider the need for objectives in managerial development.

> The experience of a medium-sized life insurance company is instructive in this instance. The company saw during the late 1950s and early 1960s market opportunities for new forms of life insurance and undertook an aggressive growth program. Since it had operated with a lean management structure, it had avoided management development that would have provided a cadre of qualified managers to meet the continuing and expanding need for managers in the company. As a result,

the top management raided the ranks of competitors to obtain qualified managers to fill the new managerial positions opened up through anticipated growth. To attract managers from outside the firm, premium compensation packages had to be offered them. The lack of attention to management development goals consistent with other goals of the firm had these results:

1. Overhead costs exceeded competitors' because of the high compensation costs for the newly hired managers.
2. Morale of managers who had been with the firm declined, because attractive openings were filled from the outside rather than from within. Further, the compensation given outsiders created pay inequities with older personnel.
3. While highly qualified individuals were attracted to the firm, the integration of their duties into those of others took several years of subpar performance as the system was being shaken down.
4. During the shakedown period of low performance, competitors made rapid strides in entrenching themselves in the markets originally attractive to the firm and the rationale for the growth it sought.

This example provides support to the Drucker thesis that lack of attention to one key area can have deleterious effects upon subsequent achievement of growth and profit goals. A balance among areas is needed. If growth had not been sought, the problems would have been less serious. When sought, however, a consistency between the growth goal and other key areas was required.

While Drucker first presented these ideas in 1954, some of the 1980s criticisms of management reflect a failure to follow his precepts. For some managers, narrow attention to maximizing short-term financial ends have left their organizations ill-prepared to weather economic downturns such as during 1981–82 or, in the long run, adversity generated by well-balanced competitors such as Woolco's failure compared with K-Mart's success. While managers can maximize profits for a while, inattention to building resources for the future of their organizations leaves them vulnerable.

Drucker's themes are logically attractive, have anecdotal evidence to support them, and have been used by a number of firms. Cyert and March's (1963, 40) research-based theory of organization supports the idea. They observe that "we can represent organizational goals reasonably well by using five different goals." Cyert and March explain the emergence of multiple goals as emanating from members of a coalition powerful enough to force the organization to attend to these goals, rather than set forth by top management. In the third chapter, attention is given to those coalition and goal formation processes.

GOALS OR CONSTRAINTS?

It may be uncomfortable to think of multiple goals as ends toward which to direct an organization's activities. After all, what is served if the organization maximizes its management development activity? The reason that an enterprise considers management development worthy of attention and allocation of resources at all is that it provides some assurance of the long-run viability and effectiveness of the system. But as an organizational goal, management development could not stand on its own as an area for maximization. The development of managers may be a necessary condition or a constraint that needs to be satisfied rather than an end in itself. Simon (1964) contends that it is doubtful whether decisions are generally directed toward achieving *a* goal. Rather, a whole set of constraints constitutes the goal-seeking ends. Therefore, the goal of organizational activity is to satisfy this set of constraints rather than to maximize the achievement of a single objective.

Constraints to the decisions made by a manager emerge primarily, according to Simon, from other parts of the organization rather than from the personal interests of the decision maker. Advertising managers are constrained in the amounts they will advertise by the capacity of the production facilities to provide articles for sale. Advertising to increase sales above capacity to deliver would, of course, be wasted. They may also be constrained by a budget, but the capacity constraint may be, for a period of time, just as important in their decision behavior as is their budget. In a similar way, advertising managers' decisions may be constrained by codes of ethics in the advertising profession, availability of different media types, product warranties and characteristics, truth in advertising practices, and so forth. Although some of these constraints originate from above in the organizational hierarchy, others are created by decisions in other parts of the organization (for example, production capacity) or outside the legal boundaries of the firm (for example, laws regulating cigarette advertising).

Advertising managers consider production capacity a constraint, but they have incomplete knowledge of factory schedules and warehouse inventories for the products they advertise. They cannot directly couple advertising decisions to the production constraint, but the system is at least *loosely coupled* (Simon 1964). Similarly, one measure that may be used to evaluate advertising managers is gross margins produced per dollar of advertising. But since gross margins depend on product attractiveness, price, and other selling and promotion efforts, there can be a fairly wide range of acceptable values of the measure. The advertising system, then, is loosely coupled in a hierarchical, as well as a lateral, sense to decisions made elsewhere in the system.

Goals or Constraints Have Similar Effects

Resources and attention are thus seen to be directed toward the achievement of either goals or constraints. Does it make any difference whether the area of concern is called a goal or a constraint, recognizing that the usual situation calls for attention to multiple criteria? Elion (1971, 295) states that "constraints may be regarded as an expression of management's desire to have minimum attainments or levels of performance with respect to various criteria. *All constraints are, therefore, expressions of goals.*" (Italics in original.) While Cyert and March (1963, 40) discuss five different business goals, they summarize "that the goals of a business firm are a series of more or less independent constraints." Further, Simon (1964, 20) concludes, "Whether we treat all the constraints symmetrically or refer to some asymmetrically as goals is largely a matter of linguistic or analytic convenience." Thus, in the Drucker (1954) model, one could establish profitability or some measure of it as the main goal, and measures in each of the other seven key areas as constraints to be met. Such a formulation would allow the balance Drucker calls for. It would appear, however, that few decision changes would result because of this basically linguistic reformulation. It is possible to think of (1) achieving multiple goals or (2) meeting multiple constraints or (3) achieving a single goal under multiple constraints as equivalent and alternative formulations of the same decision problem.

IDEALLY CONSTRUCTED GOALS AND OBJECTIVES

What are good goals? Is there anything about their characteristics that would allow them to be more useful? There are two aspects of this question. One of them involves the nature of the goals themselves, that is, the content of the statements. A second aspect is the processes and conditions surrounding the establishment of the goals. Papers by Latham and Yukel (1975) and Hall (1975) reviewed the research literature providing support to the following concepts. These are modified by the strategic level findings of Quinn (1980). Since there are a number of individual studies that analyze the characteristics of goals and goal setting, these studies provide a starting point for more intensive investigation of these phenomena.

Goal Content

With respect to the content of the goal, *realistic* goals are more relevant toward influencing behavior than are those established on the basis of a whim. Although more difficult goals or goal levels have a beneficial impact upon performance, the establishment of goal levels considerably in excess of anything yet achieved causes organizational participants to regard the goals as irrelevant and impossible. As a consequence, *difficult* but *achievable* goals have been stated as desirable. Also important is the *logical* arrangement of the stated goal with those of others. If a sales department is to provide sales volume at a 10 percent rate above the previous year, while a second goal attempts to reduce the travel expenses of salespeople by 20 percent, the salespeople may have received two messages. One appears illogical in light of the other. The direction of behaviors expected is unclear. The clarity of goals is related to the logic of one goal in relation to others.

Goal Timing

In setting specific closed-end objectives, it is important to establish not only the content and level of future expectations but also the time period within which the objectives are to be achieved. Winning a military engagement in six months requires a quite different level of commitment than does achieving the same objective in a thirty-year war. Reasonable expectations should include an objective that specifies when the level of the objectives is to be achieved.

While most of the research upon goal setting at lower levels of an organization concludes that specific goals generate better performances than do general ones, the prior discussion on open-ended versus closed-end goals in the light of strategic level research indicates a conditional choice. Whether goals should be specific or general depends upon the nature of the situation faced. Once this amount of uncertainty, level of organization, and purpose to be served are determined, the degree of specificity can be addressed.

Goal Processes

Several processes are important to the successful establishment and management of objectives. The first of these is establishing commitment to the goals by the managers of the firm.

One of the competitive advantages that the Japanese have developed over the years has been their emphasis upon product quality. More recently, a renewed interest in higher quality has resulted in many improvement efforts on the part of American manufacturers. The president of one company has "quality second to none" as one of his corporate goals. He vividly exhibits his commitment to this goal by spot-checking the "reject baskets" during his periodic walks around the plant. By initiating actions on the spot to provide preventive remedies, he visually demonstrates his commitment and expectations to the whole organization.

If encouragement is not given to goal achievement, or if goals are simply ignored by managers after establishment, little behavior change can be expected. Encouragement of, constant attention to, and use of goals by superiors are seen as primary prerequisites to acceptance of goals by subordinates. To some extent, the training of managers in goal setting and in the use of goals can be useful in generating this commitment on their part to use them not only for themselves but also for their subordinates.

Using participative processes in establishing goals aids in developing better goals, better knowledge of them, and later attention to achieving them. Chief executive officers new to the company they are expected to lead cannot just draw upon their general knowledge of management and operations of other firms as a basis for establishing objectives that will be useful to the enterprise. They do not know enough about the firm. Even managers promoted from within need the knowledge and support of all the people they can muster in order to survive, let alone excel. Thus, involving a wide spectrum of managers in establishing objectives is important. At lower levels of the organization, a similar participative approach can provide the same benefits.

Upon being promoted to chairwoman and chief executive officer of a consumer and building products firm, Jennifer James set as her first priority the establishment of corporate goals for the company. The CEO consulted the firm's investment bankers about the "best" firms in American industry. From that report, she established a 25 percent return on invested capital as the corporate goal. This goal was never achieved under her leadership, partly because she consulted with no one within the firm. Her base of knowledge and support came from outsiders not responsible for achievement. Further, the competitive situation that the firm faced did not allow sufficient margins or a low enough capital base to achieve the "best" returns. Her replacement undertook a participative approach to goal setting to improve the potentials for success.

Successful goals have been set without participative means. Some observers contend it is not necessary to be participative where strong leadership exists. Yet, strength in leadership stems from a willingness of followers to follow. Participation in goal setting improves willingness.

SUMMARY

The purpose of this initial chapter is to introduce the underlying concepts of goals and the processes of setting both goals and their closely related derivatives: objectives. Organizations do not survive very long if their activities are aimless. Without goals, any behavior is acceptable and no behavior is unacceptable. Goals and objectives provide the direction toward which behavior in an organization is expected to progress.

As the terms are used in this book, the difference between a goal and an objective lies in their degree of specificity. A goal is a general statement: an open-ended purpose. Goals are useful in thinking about what we ought to be doing without getting entangled in the details of measurement and timing. Useful in a different way is the concept of the objective which, as used in this text, is a closed-end purpose. Objectives specify the content, level, measure, and specific time period for achievement—a much more restricted idea than that of goal. It should be noted that constraints are similar in concept to goals or objectives and have much the same impact when used in managing the organization.

Setting goals is part of the planning process. Ideally, strategies are designed to accomplish goals and other short- and long-term plans are set up to further the attainment of higher-level goals. This conception shows that a strategy is a means of achieving a goal at the top level in an organization while it is an end to pursue at a lower level of an organization. This ends becoming means at a higher level pervades all levels and types of plans in an enterprise.

Achieving goals is complicated by the multiplicity of goals that are established at any level of an organization. Achieving one may be inconsistent with achieving another. Similarly, we often do not have the information, computational ability, or time to optimize goals and must 'satisfice' or do as well as we can under the conditions. Personal and organizational goals are often in conflict as well. Deviations from planned objectives are not unusual.

As noted at the beginning of this summary, we set goals to influence behavior and prevent aimlessness. In specification of objectives, we seek the same directions. Thus we take care in setting the content of the objective, the indicator used to measure what we want to achieve, the level of attainment expected, and the time frame in which we plan to achieve the objective. Each component of an objective guides behavior.

We can better set and achieve goals, furthermore, if the commitment by the manager setting the objectives is communicated to subordinates and if feedback of results in achieving goals is maintained. If a competitive atmosphere can also be maintained, interest in the task can be enhanced and goal achievement more likely met. Using goals as a normal, on-going part of managing aids in carrying out all parts of the management task: (1) making plans of what needs to be accomplished, (2) developing an organizational structure within which activity can best be directed toward achievement of goals, (3) making choices about the directions in which motivation is to be pointed, and (4) reviewing whether what has been accomplished is useful or whether what we are doing should be changed.

This first chapter is an introduction. Chapter 2 is more specific as to how the different planning and decision systems in an organization interact with the goal setting process. Chapter 3 examines the tradeoffs among rational, behavioral, and political decision processes useful in establishing goals and objectives.

2

Goal Structures

In large-scale modern organizations, there are a wide variety of interrelated planning concepts and systems. There may be corporate missions, master strategies, business charters, long-range plans, corporate policies, major programs, corporate creeds, grand designs, systems for programming, planning, and budgeting, capital investment systems, and so on. If such a mix of systems is not logically interrelated and if each of the planning activities does not serve the total, the efficiency, effectiveness, and even the viability of the enterprise come to question. The basic ideas have been expressed by Urwick (1952, 10): "Unless we have a purpose there is no reason why individuals should try to cooperate together at all or why anyone should try to organize them." To gain a better understanding of these activities, we examine the structure of goals and related planning actions.

HIERARCHY: BASIC IDEAS

One way of providing rationale to these different systems is through hierarchical placement (Simon 1969). Organisms as a whole consist of many subordinate parts, some of which are more important than others. The arm and hand are more important to overall functioning than the finger or fingernail. A complete organism consists of parts within subsystems nested within the whole. Major subparts existing within the human body include digestive, circulatory, locomotive, regulatory, and nervous systems. Parts of each system are nested within larger systems. Redundancy and interrelationships among systems exist. Some systems are higher in importance (for example, nervous and circulatory) to individual survival than others (reproductive or auditory).

The purpose of this section is to provide an explanation of the hierarchical arrangement of organizational goals. The discussion employs the concepts of nesting, importance, level, and interrelatedness to justify the logic of the ordering. Without such ordering, the logic of the network of plans is absent or not understood. Activities throughout a system can vary widely in effectiveness and efficiency. Without direction, effort tends to be pointed toward personal or professional goals achievement rather than toward organizational objectives.

Organizational Structures Exemplify Hierarchy

Most organizational structures obviously take on a hierarchical form. Structure is important, because the locus of planning, goal setting, and decision making is dependent upon the type of organizational structure in which the planning is done. Figure 2.1 presents a representation of two of the most prevalent kinds of organizational structures. The hierarchical nature of goals and subgoals is dependent upon organization hierarchy. For example, much of the planning that is performed at the product division level in the larger diversified organizations is performed at the corporate level in single-product functionally structured organizations (Galbraith and Kazanjian 1986). Additionally, there is a correspondence between the hierarchy of organizational structure and the hierarchy of strategies. The engineering managers in charge of designing electronic systems for the Chrysler Corporation are not undertaking responsibilities to shape the master strategy of the corporation. Nor is Lee Iacocca, chairman of the firm, intimately involved in the budgets, schedules, and assignments of personnel that are involved with a program to optimize power and mileage through electronics. Each organizational level has unique planning responsibilities and goals, although some systems obviously overlap several others, both laterally at one level in an organization and vertically, covering plans at several organizational levels.

Representing Hierarchy

A goal structure can be represented by a matrix, with the goals at any level of organization being noted as a row in the matrix. Each row's goals support objectives in the next higher row in the matrix. While true, this idea is incomplete, since a goal at one level does not support all goals at the next level, only some of them. Further, the

Figure 2.1 Dominant Corporate Organizational Forms (Partial Representations)

Functional: For Professionally Managed Single-Product-Line Firms

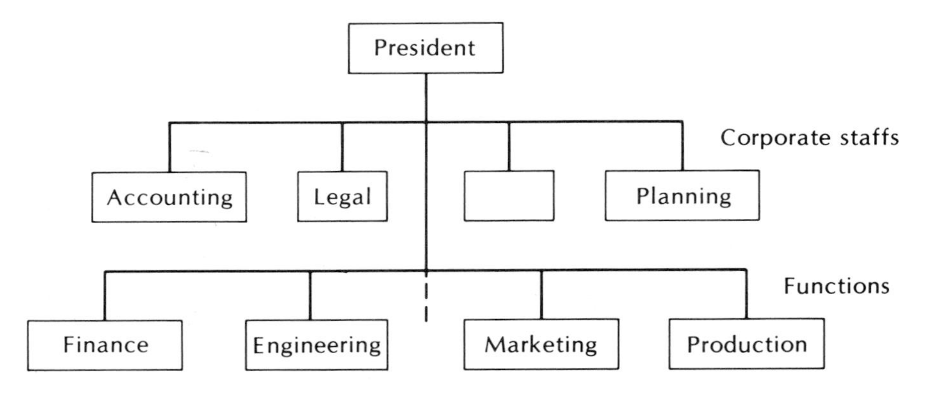

Product Divisionalized: For Multiproduct Diversified Firms

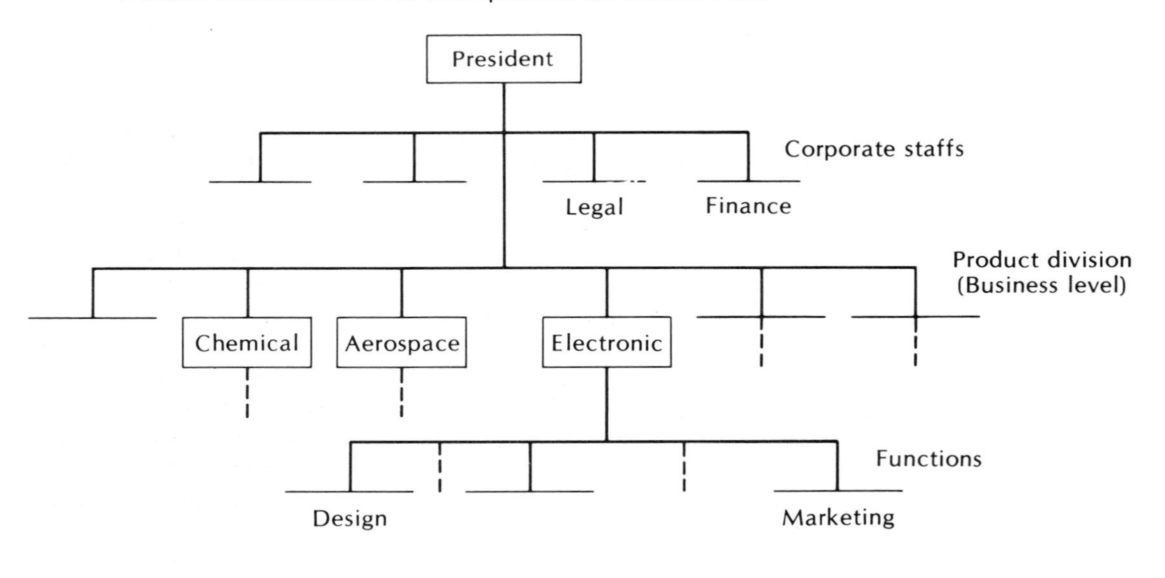

matrix assumes the form of a pyramid rather than the typical rectangular matrix.

A more accurate representation can be gleaned by examining Figure 2.2. Each goal is represented by an arch. Nested within the

Figure 2.2 Representing Hierarchy

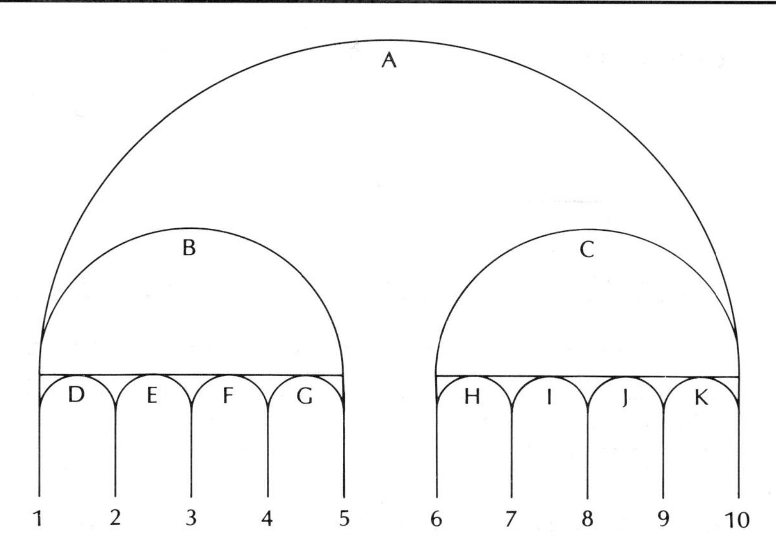

overall goal A are goals B and C. The B and C goals have no common subgoals. Thus, if goal F fails, it affects only B, not C. The goals of B and C are interrelated only as they support A. If B fails, C is unaffected except as A is influenced and if, in turn, A influences C.

E and F are supported by a common column. If column 3 fails, both E and F are first affected and then B to A, as explained previously. The goals E and F interlock as do all D through G. This representation of hierarchy has been done with goals as the example. The same kind of explanation could be made for a hierarchy of strategies, managerial levels, or organizational structure. Figure 2.2 is analogous to the organizational structure of a product divisionalized firm as shown in the lower half of Figure 2.1. A can be likened to a corporate goal. Then, B and C would be goals for different product divisions. Goals D through G would represent functional goals for product division B, and goals H through K would represent functional goals for product division C.

In early July 1983, the president and CEO of TWA was considering a $4.5 million investment to automate the baggage handling of the airline's St. Louis hub (*Business Week,* 25 July 1983). At a time when TWA was losing millions needed for huge investments to replace its aging plane fleet, it was experiencing a decline in domestic passenger traffic. St. Louis and TWA were being bested by competition using

> Chicago or Dallas (or both) as their hubs. Further, productivity at other lines had been improved by more favorable labor contracts than TWA had been able to achieve. The $4.5 million investment is obviously related to the productivity goal, which is also served by the failed labor negotiations with its unions. The investment could possibly be better applied to new planes for better domestic services, revenues, and perhaps profitability. This one investment is then related to others at the hierarchical level (labor negotiations and traffic generation) and to higher-level goals of productivity and profitability.

The commonalities of hierarchy for organization, management, goals, and strategy are shown in Table 2.2 on page 41. The table was prepared to summarize the analysis of this chapter, but it might be useful to examine it at this point to preview what is coming and the interrelationships among these parts.

HIERARCHY OF OBJECTIVES

At the highest level, that of legitimacy, social institutions are sanctioned, encouraged, and constrained, and even eliminated by the larger society of which they are a part. The system of private property ownership in the United States is sanctioned and encouraged because of the proposition that systems of public ownership of the means of production and distribution of goods and services are not as consistent with the fundamental concepts of freedom of individual choice and efficiency as is private enterprise. The totality and the individual units of private enterprise are expected to contribute to furthering the goals of society. Since, however, there often are unintended dysfunctional consequences of any activity, society constrains activities of its organizations to minimize undesired effects. Pollution standards are established, discrimination in employment is forbidden, hours of work are regulated, and so on, while at the same time loan assistance is available, trade treaties favorable to U.S. firms are negotiated, and the basic economic system is developed.

Guiding Philosophy

Within the framework of sanctions, encouragement, constraints, and prohibitions imposed by society as a whole, the contributions that a particular organization may want to make and the way it will operate to make them can be established. A high-fashion dress manufacturer may want to bring excitement, uniqueness, and flair to its customers, with protection and warmth as minor factors. Custom-designed dresses are considered means of satisfying these intended values. The managerial beliefs of what is important are basic to setting guiding philosophies. If the motto "To be the best manufacturing firm in the world" guides the behavior at Lincoln Electric, it is more than an advertising program; it is an expressed value that governs and influences. Crown Cork and Seal has enunciated its beliefs, including, "A business enterprise does not exist solely for the benefit of any one group, neither customers, nor stockholders, nor employees, nor public, but that the benefits for all groups must be in balance and that the resulting benefits are the products of a well-run business" (Higginson 1956, 17).

Organizational philosophy may be codified in the form of creeds that state the principles, beliefs, and important values to which the organization ascribes. Corporate creeds often sound moralistic and close to the principles of free enterprise, as they well might, since it is at the philosophical level that the relation between the firm's intellect and that of society's is closest. Indeed, if the White House under President Nixon had followed precepts more closely aligned with those philosophies originally developed in the U.S. Constitution, Watergate and its subsequent consequences would more likely have been avoided.

Many admirable guiding philosophies for corporations have been developed and serve as the underlying interface of these firms with society's expectations of them. Such philosophic statements and their implementation through subsequent planning processes serve in guiding the firm's behavior in an intended manner and similarly serve the larger constituency outside the firm's boundaries. While some managers may hold that the development of such general creeds are futile, time-wasting exercises, the self-image of the firm and its character can be established at this highest level and is important from that viewpoint. If this step of establishing the guiding philosophy is omitted, the link between social expectations and how the firm plans to service this highest role can be lost.

Establishing creeds and the philosophic role of the firm can thus provide an important beacon to its personnel. It also establishes the base for specification of corporate objectives. When the guiding philosophy is viewed as a mere public relations ploy, it confuses the corporate self and generates cynicism within. If managers are allowed to deviate widely from corporate precepts, the believability of top management is brought into question by those within and external to the firm.

The response of top management in firms caught in illegal or socially undesirable actions typically is that some subordinate was not following company policy and that top management was unaware of the activities. Such explanations are not enough for many critics of firms undertaking, for example, illegal payoffs or price fixing. If top management is unable to ensure that its participants follow the law, let alone its own creeds, critics question whether top management either looks the other way or is lax in its leadership.

Establishing and implementing guiding philosophies that set forth the expectations of firm members in meeting the organization's role in society is useful in establishing the corporate self and, when properly implemented, helps avoid undesirable actions of its members. In addition, guiding philosophies form the base upon which relevant corporate objectives may be set.

Corporate Goals

At the overall corporate level, objectives of publicly held firms are stated most frequently in financial terms. Sales and sales growth, profit and profit growth, cash flow, earnings per share and its growth, coupled with dividend payment policy, stock appreciation, maintenance of major stockholder control, and so on, are the areas in which corporate goals have been established. In addition to financial goals whose contents and level are of most interest to stockholders and corporate managers, whose compensation may be dependent on them, corporate-level goals may also address objectives of interest to other legitimate constituencies of the enterprise. At least one firm stated as its overriding goal, "to maximize the satisfaction of our employees." Profit was considered only as a constraint, enough being sought to keep the firm solvent. Major attention was given to providing comfortable, unstressful, participative, enjoyable work surroundings. The company was so successful in achieving employee satisfaction that it almost went bankrupt.

Goals of organizations closely controlled by a few stockholders may reflect the personal objectives of their owners. The overriding objective of the owner of a retail store was to leave an inheritance to his children. Tax laws severely constrained his inheritance goal, so that the form and operation of the business were altered considerably from what would have happened if he merely sought to maximize profits.

Even in publicly held firms, the importance that top management may place on certain values will often emerge as corporate goals. Dr. Land, who founded Polaroid Corporation, was observed to seek technologically difficult product development and sale as much as profits. Thus, personal values at times emerge as corporate ends to be achieved.

Another dimension to corporate goals is attention given to other stakeholders in the fruits of the system. Some, such as unions or governmental agencies, impose constraints on the enterprise as a whole. These constraints are attended to, require resources, and need to be balanced just as any other goal, as we noted in Chapter 1. In still other areas, such as equal opportunity employment, the firm may exercise discretion in advance of governmental imposition of goals to establish its own objectives in that area.

Complementary Nonfinancial Goals

Corporate-level goals in some firms consist primarily of financial objectives. This is particularly true of conglomerate firms built from a series of acquisitions of businesses that have little technological or marketing relation to each other. The major common thread running through the subordinate organizations of a conglomerate is financial. Such firms may also benefit from a statement of a guiding philosophy, but corporate-level goals remain basically financial. It is at the level of the acquired businesses that multiple objectives in Drucker's sense are established in a conglomerate. Since each business is unrelated, the content and level of each of these goals in each of the businesses are, and probably should be, different.

In contrast, the corporate level of a single-product firm tends to establish multiple objectives for the whole corporation. Similarly, firms that diversify their product lines consistently in a marketing, technological, and production sense need to establish multiple goals at the corporate level, since the common thread throughout all of their businesses extends considerably beyond mere financial factors. It is, then, the single product or diversifier with common activities throughout its businesses that follows the Drucker scheme for the whole corporation.

Corporate Balance in Objectives

Multiple objectives need to be balanced to remove potential inconsistencies among them. The following example uses only financial criteria, but similar analyses could be made for other kinds of goals. Closed corporate goals cannot be established independently of each other. Consider only two objectives:

- 4 percent increase in sales volume per year for ten years
- 15 percent increase in profits per year for ten years

Unless there are remarkable economies of scale or terribly inefficient past operations, the profit increases seem high relative to the sales goal. For most businesses, these two goals would be incompatible. A sustained 5 or 6 percent increase in profits per year, given a 4 percent sales growth, might approach a reasonable balance.

Overall goals not only need to be consistent with each other but also need to be consistent with the master strategy of the firm. The master strategy supposedly follows from corporate goals as a means of accomplishing them. For an established organization, it is not easy to change the master strategy quickly, although it can be done over time. If 15 percent per year return on investment after taxes is set as a major objective, and the master strategy has placed the firm in forest products, then corporate goal and master strategy inconsistencies appear to exist. Forest product companies have rarely, if ever, been able to approach a 15 percent return on investment. The goal is unrealistic in light of the master strategy.

> Greyhound Corporation's chairman, John W. Teets, has established an 18 percent return on equity as an eventual goal (*Business Week*, 25 July, 1983). For three years through 1982, the firm managed a 13.8 percent return. One of the conglomerate's poorer performing businesses was its Armour meat packing division, which contributed only $13 million of the $103 million in 1982 profits. Although many actions had been tried in the Armour division to improve its position, it remained a drag upon achieving improvement in corporate-level profitability. In 1983 Greyhound agreed to sell Armour to ConAgra, Inc., for $166 million. Greyhound intends to use the proceeds of the sale to acquire another business more closely related to its goal. Greyhound changed its strategy of what businesses it intends to be in to accommodate its return on equity goal. Conversely, it could have retained Armour, thereby keeping its same strategy, and lowered the level of its objective to provide consistency between goals and strategy.

The process of setting goals and establishing strategies, then reevaluating goal levels and readjusting strategies, occurs from top to bottom. Accommodation of strategy to goals and vice versa provide management with the means to integrate operations at all levels to objectives sought at top management levels. Balance among objectives not only is important at any one level but also is important between goals and strategy at one level and between adjacent levels of an organization.

Master Strategy, or Strategy at the Corporate Level

The design of a firm's master strategy is a visionary projection of the central and overriding competitive concepts on which the organization is based. Henry Ford envisioned the "people's car" and embodied this central idea into a business strategy that resulted in the Model T Ford. If the railroads had not been in the "railroad business"

(Leavitt 1960) but had stated a master strategy in the form of "to provide rapid, safe, low-cost transportation of goods and people at intercity distances," they may have been able to thrive and prosper by entering airline, truck, bus, and barge modes of transportation. This statement of master strategy would have kept them out of urban mass transport and overseas shipping, but it would have prevented the tunnel vision and the resulting overconcentration on a particular, limited mode of transport. It would have allowed consideration of alternate business strategies that encompassed other means of accomplishing the basic need for transportation. In fairness, however, rail strategies were constrained by antitrust legislation.

A master strategy, then, should not focus on what the firm is doing in terms of products and markets currently served, but rather upon the services and utility that their products provide. A vacuum tube performs certain functions in amplification and conversions of electrical current. By focusing attention upon tubes rather than on the functions they provide, the vacuum tube manufacturers were outflanked by semiconductor firms that ultimately provided lighter, smaller, more reliable, and cheaper means of providing the same functions. Cooper and Schendel (1976) found that during technological change, companies that were leaders in the old technology were rarely leaders in the new one. In contrast with this research, however, IBM, a leader in punch card technology, became the dominant computer manufacturer. If the old IBM is viewed as providing means for data storage and manipulation rather than as leasing tabulating equipment, the transition to computers, typewriters, software systems, office systems, and copiers becomes more understandable. The role of the master strategy is to provide a basis of the firm's unique ability for competition using existing products and markets. At the same time, the master strategy provides flexibility of outlook for the creative efforts of individuals in the organization to seek new and expansive methods through new products, new systems, and new customer groups. Thus, a master strategy ought to provide a conceptual framework for renewal and growth as well as health in its present operations.

To be viable over long periods, the master strategy must also be viable in the light of environmental conditions. While Granger (1964, 68) reports a successful master strategy of a firm making seals as "to stop the leaks of the world," it is doubtful that a hat firm seeking "to cover and protect the heads of American men" would prove as viable. Until recently, the American male has increasingly been going hatless. Providing a service that is becoming obsolete because of changing tastes and habits is inconsistent with environmental conditions. Yet, predicting the environmental viability of a master strategy over time is extremely hazardous. Who can predict that a new cheap plastic cannot be developed and produced to be used in stopping leaks under a wide variety of conditions of pressure, temperature, corrosion, and so on? This question raises the more general question of, How permanent is any set of needs in society? While nutrition, health, and other needs appear basic, the form of technology and products to service them can and has changed over time.

Rather than the utility and service basis for a master strategy, some firms have successfully relied upon a technology that has many applications. Corning Glass Works has extensive expertise in glass technology that can be used in a wide variety of products serving a variety of consumer and industrial requirements. Although strategies based upon a single technology (for example, the steam locomotive) are subject to risk as technology changes, an extensive technology with a variety of products serving many needs is less subject to such risk. General Motors' master strategy has as its core the exploitation of motors energized by liquid hydrocarbons (Sloan 1964). Although this scheme has generated substantial success, its future is clouded by the potential shortages of hydrocarbons. In the late 1980s, it might appear that a master strategy based upon a glass rather than a hydrocarbon motor technology would be more consistent with environmental conditions.

A logical master strategy must be consistent not only with environments but also with the internal capabilities of the organization. A strategy "to provide safe, low-cost means of personalized air transport for personal and business use" appears consistent with the design, production, and marketing capabilities of Piper Aircraft. Conversely, a statement "to provide vehicles for aboveground or sea transport" is a much broader statement that could imply military, space, and airline transport products. Since the functional requirements of such vehicles are so different from the capabilities inherent in providing light aircraft, the master strategy for a company employing such a statement would appear rhetorical and pompous, rather than a realistic guide to the products and services that Piper could reasonably hope to offer. Too broad a statement of a master strategy runs the risk of being inconsistent with capabilities. Too narrow a statement runs the risk of being made obsolete by changing environmental technology, tastes, customs, and laws.

Corporate Strategy and Business-Level Goals

It is at the level of a separate line of business—the business unit divisional level—that corporate management will be interested in establishing multiple objectives. This level in the organization is the second level shown in the bottom half of Figure 2.1. Chapter 1 noted that Drucker (1954) proposes eight key areas in which results expected should be established if long-run success is to be achieved: (1) market standing, (2) innovation, (3) productivity, (4) physical and financial resources, (5) profitability, (6) manager performance and development, (7) worker performance and attitude, and (8) public responsibility. Each business unit would develop separate and different levels of results to be achieved and different time frames within which to accomplish them. In other words, although the open-ended goals might be similar for each business unit, the closed-end objective would differ from one line of business to another.

The goals from each business are expected to contribute to overall goals and the implementation of the master strategy. One firm's master strategy included the policy that only high-quality products would be produced. In one corporate acquisition, the company received a product line that was sold on a price basis and had one of the lowest quality levels in the industry. An immediate objective set for the new business was to achieve the highest quality level of all its major competitors. This corporate policy not only generated a quality goal but also necessitated changes in the plans and policies of the acquired business to make its strategy consistent with the corporate goal of quality.

Effects of Division Strategy on Its Goals

Although each product division is expected to contribute to corporate goals, each does so differently. In an aging line of business near the end of its product life cycle, the goal for physical resources might reasonably be to reduce overall investments by 10 percent (exclusive of depreciation) during the next year. Conversely, for a business unit experiencing rapid growth, the next year's physical resource goal might be to add capacity to take care of projected sales for the next three years.

The point to be made is that the goals of a business unit are supposedly developed from overall corporate strategy. Then, the business strategy is developed from its goals. The contention, here, however, is that business goals set without reference to the business strategy, or variations of it that could be established, may result in a mismatch between the goals and the strategy. The same point was made with respect to corporate goals and master strategy by the Greyhound example. The top-down approach to (1) establishing goals and then (2) establishing strategy most often does not stop there. After a strategy is developed, it is evaluated to see whether it can meet the goals previously set. If it could exceed them, the goals tend to be readjusted upward. If for some reason it cannot meet preestablished goals, the goals may be readjusted downward. This process of setting goals, establishing strategy, reevaluating goals and then strategy continues in a cascading fashion until satisfactory and consistent agreement between the two is reached.

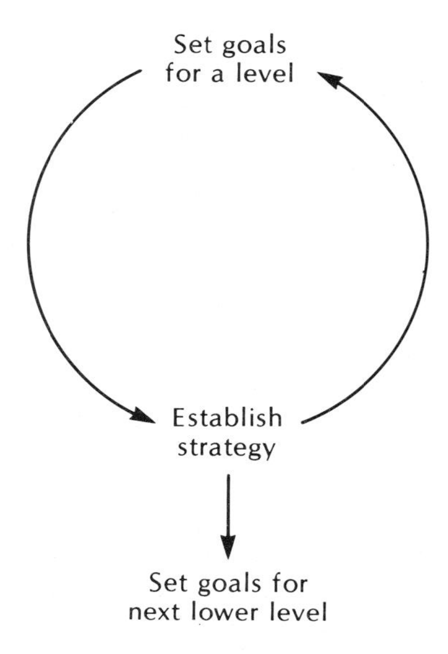

Since the power of corporate executives tends to be relatively high, division general managers tend to be pushed toward achieving ever higher levels of results. For some types of businesses, this is realistic. For others, it is not. A number of portfolio models for the describing business-level strategies have been created. Hofer and Schendel (1978) provide an explanation and evaluation of them. Most are multifactored models weighted to provide a judgment about (1) the relative attractiveness of the industry in which the business competes and (2) the relative competitiveness of the home business in that market. The basic portfolio idea originated in the Boston Consulting firm's growth-share matrix since elaborated on by (1) GE in collaboration with the McKinsey Company, (2) the Shell directions policy matrix, and (3) the Hofer Product Life Cycle matrix. See Hofer and Schendel (1978) for a complete description of each.

Employing the GE screen as an example of a portfolio model to display the position of the firm relative to its competitors and its industry relative to others, we analyze one of Drucker's goals, market standing, in each cell of the resulting matrix in Table 2.1. There is insufficient information from the position display to establish definitely for any specific business what its goals should be. From the display alone, we can develop only general tendencies. For example, for a business in the high-competitiveness column, there may be a number of combinations of reasons that the firm is strong relative to its competitors. While high relative market share (a measure of Drucker's market standing goal) is one factor used in developing the business's competitiveness, a number of other factors (usually ten to twelve) are employed to determine the relative competitiveness of a business. Consequently, the suggested "maintain share in all market segments" as a possible goal for a business in the high-high cell of Table 2.1 is a general statement and would need more information before being used for a specific business. (Much of the specific information required for this choice exists in the backup data prepared to place the firm in the high-high category of the screen in the first place, i.e., the factors used to evaluate competitiveness, the factor rankings and weightings that provide the basis for the high-competitiveness judgment.) Chapter 4 uses these ideas for a specific business.

The same warning is relevant to the industry attractiveness division. For a business in the low industry attractiveness–high business competitiveness cell, we have a suggested goal of maintaining share in the most attractive segments. This suggestion stems from the diversity of attractiveness any industry can exhibit—some segments

Table 2.1 The GE Portfolio Matrix: Possible Market Standing Goals (e.g., Market Share)

Industry Attractiveness	Business Competitiveness: *High (A)*	*Medium (B)*	*Low (C)*
High (1)	Maintain all segments	Maintain or increase: all segments	Increase for most attractive segments
Medium (2)	Maintain all segments	Maintain or increase in attractive segments	Maintain or decrease for cash flow
Low (3)	Maintain in most attractive segments; decrease in less attractive	Maintain	Maintain for potential divestiture or decrease for phaseout

growing, some declining with cutthroat competition, and so forth. On balance, some are not worth being in and share can be harvested. In others we should maintain share or even pick up share if competitors exit.

Given all these caveats in the use of Table 2.1, what information can the table provide? First, for businesses in which an investment strategy is called for (A1, A2, B1), maintaining or increasing share is suggested in all segments in which the firm is participating. Second, for businesses operating on the lower left to upper right diagonal (C1, B2, A3), maintaining or increasing share for only attractive segments while decreasing share in unattractive segments is the level of market shares called for. In the remaining lower right cells (C2, C3, B3), a maintaining share goal for divestiture or reducing share to phase out the business are appropriate goals for market standing.

It is readily recognized that setting multiple goals for ongoing businesses can be time-consuming and complex. A separate table similar to Table 2.1 is appropriate for each of the eight areas in which objectives should be established if one wishes to generate the general type of objective developed in Table 2.1. Alternately, one could go to the specifics of each business and establish goals directly without reference to these generalities, although these can provide a general check upon the specific goals established.

Portfolio Models and Business-Level Goals

How does the knowledge of business position in a portfolio matrix inform us about setting business goals? First, each of the several product divisions in a diversified firm will likely be in a different position in the matrix, so that different expectations of their results should be evident. The same growth rates and profit rates for all businesses cannot be expected. To fine-tune business objectives, then, consideration from both the master strategy and the business's strategic position is relevant. If it is not possible (even by altering strategies and operations at the business level) to adequately contribute to corporate-level goals, top management will need to consider changing corporate strategy to exit from the low-achieving business or to lower the level of expected corporate goals.

Second, each of the businesses in a diversified firm will contribute differently to the corporation. A relatively new, fast-growing business will represent potential for the future but will, in growth, consume investments for product development and for establishing brand name, plant and equipment, and working capital. A large mature business, on the other hand, may require little investment, will contribute large profits (although not necessarily high margins), and will generate cash in excess of its needs. The goals expected from each will reflect these differences.

The role of those managing the master strategy is to juggle the individual businesses to ensure that overall corporate-level goals are met. Each line of business can best contribute in different ways.

Third, the position of a business changes over time in response to (1) its own efforts to become more competitive, (2) the actions of competitors, and (3) the maturation of the industry. An attractive business neglected may move to an unattractive position because the industry has become less attractive while competitors have made inroads on the target business position.

Functional Objectives

Large-scale group endeavors require a division of efforts so that each part of the job required to accomplish overall goals can be performed more efficiently. At some level of most organizations, a functional organizational form is found. The grouping consists of individuals assigned a common specialized task on the basis of the kind of work performed. Examples of functional organizations are engineering, production, marketing, finance, and manufacturing. In a retail store, the functions are buying, inventory, stock control, display, selling, credit, and delivery. In a multiproduct firm, there may be separate parallel functional organizations. For example, a company producing pumps, motors, and valves might have separate engineering organizations for each of these products as well as separate production and marketing organizations.

The goals of each functional department are fashioned by the nature of its environment, which consists not only of societal expectations, and the modern technologies of the function, which may have been developed any place in the world, but also of the strategy of the business of which it is a part. In addition, the environment of any particular department, such as engineering, is constrained or influenced by the activity and goals of other functional organizations with which it interacts. Most frequently, these interactions occur at the same organizational level and within the same product line of business. For example, in a company producing pumps, motors, and valves, the engineering organization designing valves may be little influenced by the production or marketing organizations working with pumps. But within the valve division itself, the engineering of the valves, the preciseness of engineering standards, and the relevance of these standards to the operation of the valve greatly influence the ability of the manufacturing department to produce and assemble these valves so that they will work.

Thus, if the engineering department provides a rough engineering design, the manufacturing department would spend considerable time adjusting and filing down parts, forcing assemblies, and so on, in order to make the valve parts fit together and work properly. Whether the engineering department should attempt to achieve preciseness in design depends to some extent on the overall business strategy and the goals of the marketing department, as well. If a design is expected to sell in large volumes over long periods of time, the engineering department could be expected to expend much time and energy in engineering, drafting, pilot and experimental productions, and testing before the finalized design is sent to manufacturing for large-scale production. On the other hand, if the valve is specially ordered and will be produced only once, the amount of engineering time that would be economical to devote to the valve would be relatively less, even though such a design would require more adjustments in production. Thus, the functional goal of degree of design preciseness for an engineering department depends upon its constraints and relationship to other departments, that is, marketing and production, as well as to the overall objectives of the valve business itself. If general management is developing the business as a specialized valve manufacturer, the goals of the production, marketing, and engineering departments would be considerably different than if a mass market strategy were being pursued.

Although the functional organization's goals are dependent upon those of the parent business and other functional units with which it interacts, the importance of different functions varies by the particular positioning of the business in the portfolio matrix. If, for example, the valve business is classified in a relatively weak competitive position in a growing market, then the business decision may be to attempt to improve its position to a highly competitive one before the market growth starts to ebb. The marketing department's strategy under such an overall business strategy would involve considerable promotion, selling effort, advertising, and so on, in order to achieve an increased market share goal. Thus, the relevant importance of marketing under these conditions would be rather high compared with what it would be if the firm were classified as highly competitive.

If the product is noncompetitive in a mature market, the business may be attempting to find a particular market niche in which it can become dominant. It would wish to avoid direct competition with industry leaders but remain in the business by finding an area of it in which the leaders do not compete. At one time, for example, American Motors was attempting to distinguish itself from the three big car manufacturers by focusing upon small cars while the big three were pursuing large car sales. Under such a product differentiation mode, the firm attempts to avoid head-on competition with leaders. It focuses its advertising upon groups of customers whose needs are met by the differentiated product, and its resources are differentiated rather than being the same as competitors. The goals of the engineering department are to design a different small car rather than a better big car. Goals and the requirements for behavior within functions are different, then, depending on how the business involved is positioned in the portfolio matrix and the strategic choices made about that position.

SUMMARY

This chapter has shown that a *single* goal does not very well represent the kinds of objectives that organizations actually seek. Rather, organizations, both their parts and their total, each seek multiple goals. Their objectives and subobjectives are influenced by the larger system of which they are a part (see Table 2.2). Overall guiding principles and the master strategy of the firm are the links that the firm has to society as a whole. These links fashion the overall objectives of the organization. Particular kinds of business have separate and differentiated goals that are based upon its stages in the product life cycle or upon its position in a portfolio model. Functional goals are dependent upon the objectives and the type of business in which the organization of which it is a part is undertaking.

Table 2.2 Goal Structures and Hierarchy

Organizational Hierarchy	Managerial Hierarchy	Goal Hierarchy	Strategic Hierarchy
Board of directors Corporate offices	Founder, chairman, president	Economic and social values and balance among them →	Guiding philosophy
Corporate	President	Overall goals Corporate objectives →	Master strategy
Business unit and corporate	President, division manager	Business goals →	Business strategies
Functions and business unit	Function manager	Functional goals →	Functional strategies

Furthermore, functional objectives, as the objectives of any other unit in an organization, are dependent on and constrained by the activities and goals of other units with which they interact. Inconsistency among goals at a particular organizational level and friction among subsystems exist because of a lack of clarity about how behavior in one sub-system affects that in others. There is an imperfect mesh among the goals of functional departments. This inconsistency may require a constant adjustment of goals and constraints as each system mutually interacts with others.

Goal structures of a unit are influenced not only vertically from above and below but also in a horizontal or lateral sense by the constraints and goals of other units with which they interact.

RELEVANCE OF GOAL STRUCTURES

What does all this mean to managers? How can they use it? Several conclusions can be drawn.

In complex organizations, several distinct but interrelated hierarchies exist:

- goal hierarchy
- strategy hierarchy
- managerial hierarchy
- organizational hierarchy

Table 2.2 shows the correspondence of these levels. In addition, it shows the flow between goals and strategies at different levels. As we have previously mentioned, strategy at any one level feeds back in a cascading maneuver to the goals at that level. To show that reverse feedback effect, the arrows in Table 2.2 would need to have their reverse shown as well.

In addition to vertical hierarchies, there are horizontal relationships among goals, strategies, managers, and organizational units at any one level. At the general manager of an autonomous product division level, the horizontal relationships to other product divisions in the corporation often are not very important and do not need much coordinated effort. (This would be modified if buying and selling between divisions were common.) At the functional level of the organization, however, the goals and strategies of any function affect every other and tend to interlock. As noted, the goals at the functional level do and must be interrelated. At least, goals of other interlocking functions constitute constraints.

Looking vertically, then, managers want to assure themselves that their strategy is consistent with their goals and that their goals best service the strategies of their superiors. In the downward direction, they use their subordinates' goals as indicators of how well they can carry out their strategy. Thus, coordination of their efforts through negotiating their goals (and often advising on their strategies) is required.

Looking horizontally, managers need to assure themselves that their goals are consistent with those of others, to the extent they interact. Functional managers most often find this a problem, which will be resolved in many instances by self-coordination with other managers. Superiors of several interdependent units, however, also need to assure themselves that subordinate goals and strategies are designed to mesh in a coordinated manner.

Hierarchy surrounds us. National governments control regional and state governments, which in turn control governments of cities and municipalities. The computer operating system controls the application program and the subroutine operations. Higher-level goals of organizations take precedence over lower objectives. Hierarchy describes a means of making sense out of the cornucopia of goals that otherwise might be difficult to differentiate. Together with the materials in the first chapter of the book, hierarchy provides a base with which we can now examine social and economic goals in the next two chapters.

3

Rational and Political Perspectives in Establishing Objectives

RATIONAL PROCESSES

The last chapter showed the relationships among goals and strategies at various levels in a multiproduct firm. In addition to establishing objectives and strategies, an organizational unit also may engage in long-range planning and yearly planning or budgeting. In a rational top-down relationship among these several systems, the following diagram may be helpful.

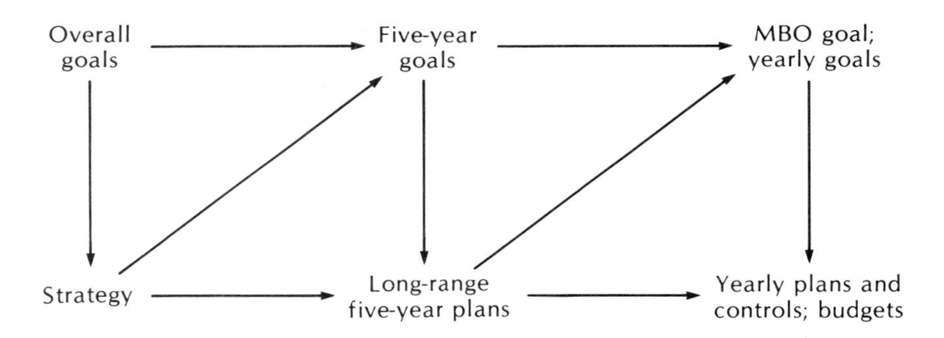

Overall goals are a basis for development of strategy and for establishing what long-range goals should be accomplished within a particular time frame. Five years has been used as the interval for long-range planning because that is typical for U.S. organizations, although longer and shorter periods are not uncommon. During the five-year period, the overall goal represents a target at which the five-year goals aim. The overall organizational goal might state a 12 percent return on investment, and a five-year plan might seek intermediate levels of return on investment to get from where the firm is actually operating to where its overall goals and grand design dictate.

Long-range plans constitute a set of anticipated activities to couple strategy to present operations. A yearly budget and goals for the short range stem from long-range plans. MBO is an approach to couple current expected results to longer-range goals.

In a completely rational system, overall goals are closely linked to overall strategy and the goals of long-range planning. In those enterprises facing a highly uncertain environment, the ability and the desirability of a tight coupling among these elements is more questionable than in firms facing little uncertainty. Thus, different organizations might link them together more or less closely, depending upon the predictability of the conditions faced.

Similarly, MBO goals and the yearly plans provide a higher specification of activity during the nearest year in a five-year plan. In contrast with such a tight coupling, some MBO goal setting and yearly budgeting are developed with less reference to long-range planning. The reason for such looseness in coupling may stem from a lack of experience in integrating from strategic goals to MBO systems. Another reason may be the disbelief that planning can be usefully translated in the firm to operationally viable action plans.

The connection between goals and operations in the systems previously described is understandably rational in intention. The overall purposes are served through the conscious development of an interrelated series of plans and objectives. Although some firms can and do approach such behavior, the complexity of large-scale organizations, together with the personal desires and interests of individuals in groups, make the task of achieving rational, optimal goals difficult. Managers who do consider optimality desirable are frustrated in achieving it. The purpose of this chapter and the next is to review some of the major findings of research directed toward a better understanding of the political rather than rational goal-setting processes. With this knowledge, managers can deal with the establishment of goals more realistically in light of the behavioral and political processes that exist in organizations (MacMillan and Jones 1986).

POWER

To accomplish this task, it is first important to recognize that power, or the ability and willingness to influence affairs in an organization, and the values held by individuals and groups can directly influence goal formation and achievement. Because the distribution of power is sometimes widespread rather than concentrated, attention to goals emanating from a number of individuals within and external to the organization may be required. The resolution of disjointed interests leads to a number of social interactions affecting the character and means for achieving objectives. Yet, certain patterns of goal groupings have been discovered. It is to these patterns that managers turn their attention if they choose to use and influence the goal processes of their organizations.

The experience of a division manager of a small conglomerate is instructive in showing how the political factors may be controlling over those of a rational nature. The division of which Don Cable was in charge sold equipment to the military through prime contractors in the aerospace industry or directly to the contracting military agency that specified the equipment for the aerospace system being built. Don was considered a young, bright, up-and-coming executive. The demand for his division's product was reaching a mature stage such that increases in the rate of orders had slowed and the expectations for the future predicted a gradual decline in sales.

At the same time, the demand for products in other divisions of the conglomerate was declining absolutely. The corporate managers were intensely involved in attempting to acquire new businesses and were looking internally for possible new product developments that could be grown into reasonable size within a five-year period. The overall reductions in sales growth of the conglomerate had also triggered attempts throughout the firm to reduce costs and to cut overhead.

Within Don Cable's division was lodged a small investment castings (lost wax process) operation that had been developed as a means of reducing machining time. Previous lack of capacity had suggested this technique as a means for the company's products to be rough sized without the need for using machining capacity. The investment castings operation lost money at a rapid rate while sales were increasing. Costs exceeded sales volume by 100 to 200 percent. Cable saw the opportunity to cut his costs to within budgeted expectations that the headquarters group had sought from him by shutting down the castings operation and purchasing the cast parts on the open market at prices comparable to the transfer sales prices. He estimated that a savings of $60,000 to $80,000 a year could be made and his cost goals substantially met by this proposed shutdown action. He recommended that the investment castings operation be discontinued.

In charge of the investment castings operation was Jack Fields, an old-timer at the company and a former division manager who had been put in charge in order to make castings a viable enterprise in its own right, perhaps becoming an independent division. Jack knew his way around the company and had many long-time friends throughout the firm, its customers, and suppliers. Jack opposed the shutting down of the castings business. He argued with Don about the probability that the business would soon be profitable in the face of increasing losses as sales increased. Jack had entrée to top executives and did not hesitate to make his feelings about the eventual health of the castings business known to them. While Jack formally reported to Don, his direct access to headquarters enabled him to bypass Don without reprisals as the headquarters executives backed the continuance of the castings business as a seed for future growth.

Jack's politicking with headquarters annoyed and ultimately enraged Don to the point that Don subsequently left the firm. The castings business had to be closed shortly after Don's departure.

In this situation, the rational choice to shut down the investment operations was overshadowed by the internal politicking that allowed Jack to prevail. The friendship coalition was able to overpower the legitimate interests of the firm.

POWER SOURCES

Every individual possesses some degree of power. The president of a large corporation may have far-ranging influence upon its direction and activity. The janitor may have only the power to perform tasks as assigned or to refuse to do so, risking the potential consequences of personal choice. Since any member can be replaced at some cost to the system, individual power is restricted. The range of power discretion among different individuals is obviously great.

Potential ability to influence is not always used in totality. The president may have the power to insist that the marketing vice-president and the marketing organization focus their activities on the goal of increasing product market share 10 percent per year over the next three years. The president may elect not to insist on such a goal, preferring that the marketing group participate with her in establishing its objectives. Potential power is not always exercised. Since power limits are somewhat fuzzy, it may be dangerous to employ one's full powers and then risk failure. The dean of a professional school in a large university, attempting to demonstrate his support, asked his faculty for a vote of confidence. When, instead, a vote of no confidence resulted, an observer noted that the dean had overestimated his limits of power to rally support.

One of the useful frameworks for discussing power sources is the French and Raven (1959) paper widely cited in this regard. They distinguish five bases of social power: reward, coercive, referent, expert, and legitimate sources. The ability to influence by providing rewards for desired behaviors constitutes the *reward* basis. Many forms of organizational rewards (for example, pay, prestige, position, perquisites, and status) may increase the influence of the individual controlling these rewards.

Coercive power stems from the ability of a given individual to influence another through punishment or threat thereof. Carrying through on threats, if behavior is unacceptable, is as important as carrying through in providing promised rewards if power is not to be eroded or lost. Since coercive threats are considered repressive to some, the use of coercive means to influence others may not be used as extensively in some societies as in others.

Referent power is the ability to influence that an individual has because of the identification another has with him or her. John F. Kennedy was able to attract members to his administration because of the aura of personality he exuded. Identification provides the individual with an effective means to incorporate, psychologically, the strength of another in him- or herself. Whether objectives to which leaders ascribe are a precondition to their obtaining referent power or whether goals are established by them after achieving power is open to question. For example, Winston Churchill, the great World War II leader, lost the election after his cause was won. Certainly, the influence of great causes and charismatic leaders go together. In any event, a manager may have numerous individuals that want to identify with her because she demonstrates admired characteristics. To the extent that managers or leaders enjoy this condition, they are able to exert referent power. Few leaders are able to freely create a charismatic condition favorable to them, however. Steve Jobs, chairman of Apple Computer, was able to develop charisma as individuals attracted to the success and the Apple lifestyle and culture tended to idolize him.

> In the election of chief of surgery for a hospital, a surgeon with the longest tenure won the election and the prestige associated with the position. After the elections, there was some rumbling among the surgical staff as the new chief made changes in the operating room and personnel assignments. This dissatisfaction was relatively minor and was soon smoothed over as the staff settled into the new routine. As time progressed, however, it became evident to doctors and staff that the chief was losing his skills as a surgeon. After one noted incident in which a simple appendectomy turned into a life-and-death case, resolved in the short run by another doctor, a rising tide of animosity on the part of the staff toward the chief surgeon became overwhelming. As small groups started to discuss the situation, a coalition opposed to the chief remaining in that role (and in surgery at all) became powerful enough to displace him. While his behaviors were admired up to the time that his degraded skills became evident, this referent power was overcome by his decline in expertise.

Expert power refers to the potential of one to influence another because of superior knowledge and expertise in a particular field. The acceptance of consultants' recommendations stems from their unique experience-based abilities. Growing knowledge and complexity prevent comprehensive knowledge of organizations and their operations. Thus, modern organizations rely on experts and expertise as a power source. A statement that "this pump will not stand up in the field under the corrosive conditions of its potential uses" will not have much influence if it comes from the advertising director with no expert knowledge of the subject. Influence to change the decision would be greater if it came from someone acquainted with both conditions and the resistance of the materials used, such as an engineer or a designer.

A final base of social power in the French and Raven framework is *legitimacy*. Individuals accede to the suggestions of others because they perceive that this action is correct. Legitimate power in organizations is associated with the *position* the individual occupies. Because he is the boss, a new salesperson follows the lead of the district sales manager. At the same time, the salesperson may not be influenced by suggestions from the chief accountant, whose position is not considered a legitimate source of power over the salesperson. Even individuals closely associated with a legitimate power can influence others, as one can observe that a call from the president's secretary gets as much attention as one from a respected associate.

Coalition Formation

Because there are diverse bases for social power in organizations, managers are able to influence others from multiple power sources. At the same time, there are competitive individuals and managers with power in the hierarchy above, beside, and below the manager. If power is relatively evenly and widely dispersed, there may be difficulty in arriving at common organizational goals and direction of effort. In a small general hospital, the surgeon, anesthesiologist, pathologist, and radiologist are individually powerful. If they do not agree on common directions for the hospital, but rather decide to pursue their individual personal and professional interests, overall organizational goals, if stipulated at all, will be served only to the extent that the personal and professional goals of the medical staff are consistent with hospital goals.

Under what conditions do coalitions form? Consider the following organization of three individuals.

	Relative Power
Art	2
Betty	3
Carl	4

Each has power, and relatively, Carl has more power than Betty or Art, and Betty has more than Art. None, moreover, possesses enough power relative to the others to dominate choices in the group. The combined relative power of any two in coalition, however, is sufficient to control group choice if they so elect. The whole group could agree to act in concert or independently if they desired, but only two need agree in order to control organizational choice. Several questions arise from this simplified example. Which coalitions under what conditions are most likely? Is relative power a meaningful concept? What is the relevance of coalition formation in organizations?

Coalition Types

Mintzberg (1979) considers coalitions consisting of members *external* to the legal boundaries of the firm and *internal* coalitions. He notes three types of external coalitions, the types being dependent upon the degree to which their power is concentrated (see Figure 3.1).

Figure 3.1 Types of External Coalitions

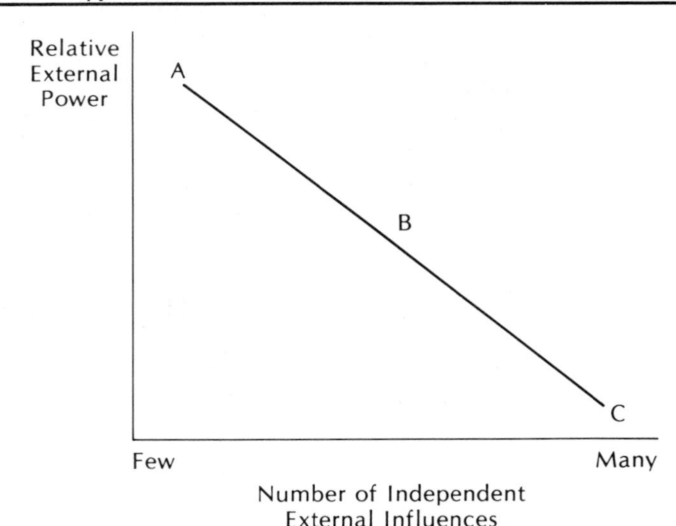

A = Dominated coalitions, concentrated power

B = Divided coalitions, divided powers

C = Passive coalitions, fragmented power

Where a relatively large number of external pressures are brought to bear upon the internal system, the external coalition is passive in nature and unable to concentrate its individual powers to influence internal operations. Conversely, a dominated coalition can exert considerable internal influence to affect goals and behavior, as International Harvester's creditors have done during the span of its operating problems. A single majority stockholder/owner who wishes to exercise her ownership rights to direct the actions of the firm is an example. Sears Roebuck as the major customer of Whirlpool Corporation can act as a dominant external coalition, whose influence Whirlpool can ignore only at substantial risk.

A few external influences sharing power constitute a divided coalition, each member of which seeks to impose its own control over the affairs of the enterprise. A divided coalition is, according to Mintzberg, midway between a dominated and a passive external coalition in terms of the power it is able to exercise in goal formulation within a firm.

Processes of External Coalitions

Table 3.1 classifies the types of activities undertaken by external coalitions to influence goal setting and behavior. The following review of activities used by external coalitions concerning foreign bribes by U.S. corporations is used as an example to define the several processes in Table 3.1 by which external coalitions influence an organization's goals and behavior. In the United States, it is considered unethical to bribe governmental, supplier, or customer officials as a means of gaining favors. In some foreign countries, in

Table 3.1 External Coalition Influence Approaches

Specificity of Influence	External Influence Methods	Examples
Low	1. Social norms	Euthanasia is bad; speeding wastes energy.
	2. Specific constraint (or norm made official)	Euthanasia is illegal; trucks must obey 55 MPH speed limit.
	3. Pressure campaign	Union strikes; boycotts by consumers.
	4. Direct access to decisions and the firm	Customer is asked to participate in cost reduction efforts.
High ↓	5. Board of directors membership	Banker participates in overall board decisions as member.

contrast, such bribes are expected and constitute a normal way of doing business. To sell airplanes in some Middle Eastern countries, bribes to a relative of the ruler grease the way for settling final contracts. At one time, there was no specific prohibition against U.S. multinationals engaging in these payoff practices. The Securities and Exchange Commission has contended, however, that U.S. firms engaging in such practices must reveal the extent of their participation in them as part of the full disclosure requirement of their financial activities for the registration and sale of their securities. The social norms of United States business practice are thus, in effect, being extended to overseas activity. Although SEC disclosure is not a specific constraint against such payoff behavior, it has much the same power as a prohibition. Once such socially unacceptable behaviors are revealed, the public pressures to discontinue them become overpowering.

Aroused Congressmembers have, upon learning of overseas payoffs by American companies, introduced legislation to make such payoffs illegal. Thus, the SEC indirect constraint can become direct through new legislation. As Table 3.1 shows, a more specific action by external coalitions is the pressure campaign. Stockholder suits and stockholder associations were initiated in attempts to force company officials involved in foreign payoffs to repay such sums to the corporation, thereby safekeeping the financial rights, supposedly, of the stockholders. In response, corporations asked auditing firms or blue-ribbon panels of outsiders to investigate the extent of corporate involvement. Similarly, some other corporations established special investigating committees of their own board of directors (supplemented by outside investigative assistance, in some cases) to study and report upon corporate involvement in foreign bribes.

The cases of foreign bribes and payoffs illustrate all of the processes that external coalitions employ in their attempts at influencing the goals and activities internal to organizations. Societal norms formed the basis of criticism, specific constraints were applied, pressure campaigns mounted, and decisions by outsiders and board members were employed. It should be noted that as more directly influential external processes were beginning to be employed, the corporations involved began to appoint their own outside investigators and blue-ribbon committees from the board of directors. In this way, it could be argued, these organizations co-opted the processes that the external coalitions could have employed. This approach may be akin to an accused appointing his or her own jury.

Internal Coalitions: The Conditions for Formation

In small organizations, chief executive officers (CEOs) may be able to establish organizational objectives and operating subgoals by retaining control over the powers invested in them by the board of directors. Although the board technically has total power within legal and environmental constraints, the part-time nature of most director memberships means that the board cannot retain for a long period the powers that incorporation provides. Most authority, however, must be delegated to the CEO in order for the system to operate. Although the board supposedly retains the power to select chief executives, set dividend policy, and determine major resource allocations and overall corporate strategy, Mace (1971) shows that the superior knowledge of chief executives allows them in most cases to obtain substantial influence over these board-reserved functions.

By establishing a relatively small number of personnel systems, strategy and planning systems, and information systems, the CEOs may be able to retain personal control to ensure that activity in the organization is directed toward the goals they select. They can reward those who follow and punish those who do not. In larger enterprises, however, formal as well as personalized control and information means are needed. The groups of individuals designing and operating the resource allocation system in a larger firm, for example, establish a power base, since the CEO must rely upon their judgments in and detailed knowledge of the resource allocation process. Top management may just be rubber-stamping investment choices made at lower levels (Bower 1972). Further, the goals of resource allocation can be subverted as lower-level managers manipulate their presentations of recommendations to satisfy their own interests rather than those established by top management and the systems designer. The mere size of organizations together with the differentiation of functions, then, tend to erode the potential power of the CEO by requiring delegation of powers to others. The sum of the parts does not equal the whole, because of the inevitable errors in division into parts and the attention to them rather than to the whole.

As an organization becomes systematized and bureaucratized, and as tasks become differentiated, the imperfect matches that are inevitable between subparts and the whole arise. As individuals seek to maximize the goals of their subparts, suboptimization occurs. In addition, the measures used may imperfectly reflect the objective being sought. In the first chapter, the behavior and decisions differences between using ROI and ROE as alternate ways of measuring profitability were discussed. Neither measure is completely adequate. Measures of subordinate goals suffer in a similar way. Suborganization interests and personal values of groups and individuals can be served instead of overall goals if subordinates have the choice of measures to be employed. Thus, in the normal course of events in complex systems, the distribution of power and influence throughout the system by delegation is an ordinary result.

Expertise required in a system is a further incubator of potential coalition formation. Although most large-scale organizations are subject to attending to the demands of its experts, hospitals, commercial research organizations, and universities consist of a large number of experts, perhaps a majority of the members in the enterprise. Because the primary impetus to the goals of such systems exist in the expert groups, the top management may be little able to exert effective power to weld the organization into a cohesive whole. Etzioni (1975) argues that the line management and staff roles are reversed in such expert-based systems. The medical staff in a hospital makes the important decisions, and the line administrative group merely provides the means for facilitating medical goals. Conversely, Mintzberg (1979) argues that the hospital board of directors, through its fund-raising functions, derives substantial power over hospital goals and operations. Perhaps initially, the prestige and status associated with board membership are sufficient to induce fund raising on the part of the board while expecting little power over internal operations in return.

At another stage of development of the hospital, in which the resources become extremely scarce, the administrative coalition (because of its cost-cutting expertise) emerges as relatively powerful vis-à-vis the board of trustees and the medical staff. Such changes in coalitions come about as the primary problems of the enterprise evolve. It reminds us of the changing conditions encountered by the transport equipment company noted previously. Its traditionally strong product development coalition gave way to accounting and finance coalitions as financial problems threatened the firm. The product development groups reemerged as powerful when the financial issues eased and as the need for product development was recognized as a central requirement in the future functioning of the enterprise.

Values, Attitudes, and Interests

The origins and changes in societal and environmental values are important to assaying the power that external coalitions and individuals within the organization will exercise. The fifth chapter is devoted to a close examination of changing values and organizational responses, but it is important at this point to show how power combines with the values and attitudes of individuals to provide understanding of the content and level of objectives sought. Earlier in this chapter, the power of three individuals was presumed known. Consider the coupling of their relative power (from whatever source) to their commitment to a set of values. The following example simplifies this problem by considering only three values, but the principles it illustrates are useful.

Relative Power of Individual		Relative Strength of Value Held		
		Honesty	*Efficiency*	*Stability*
Art	2	6	5	3
Betty	3	7	5	2
Carl	4	2	4	8

Although neither Art nor Betty has as much relative power as Carl, considering their commitments to these three values, their attitudes are more similar to each other's than to Carl's. If either of them joined Carl in a dominant coalition, the values of honesty and efficiency would suffer in periods of no slack, since Carl, as the most powerful, would be concerned with stability. Thus, to explain who would join whom in a coalition of powerful individuals, an understanding of values held is useful. The goals of the coalition of Art and Betty would in probability include a consideration of, if not maximum attention to, honesty and efficiency. Stability might be considered if it did not interfere with the achievement of the other two, that is, if there were enough resources. It should be noted here that the science of measurements for relative power and commitment to values is immature; the numbers provided in this example are hypothetical rather than realistic for what can be measured. Furthermore, the example does not consider the potential bargaining behaviors that Carl could undertake. If he could convince either Art or Betty that long-run efficiency is most consistent with the stability of operations, he might be able to convince one of them to join him. It is also at this point that the use of side payments in various forms of policy commitments, in establishing inoperative goals, and in creating status positions could come into use (Cyert and March 1963), as evidenced in the following case.

> A large manufacturing organization, preeminent in its products, had several manufacturing locations that produced end products for customers and finished parts and subassemblies for each of the other divisions. The top management concluded that each division had similar rather than distinctive capabilities. This condition resulted in

> the duplication of processes, resources, and skills, all of which were in short supply. To reduce the duplication, the top executives decided to assign each division a limited line of products so that a degree of divisional specialization and expertise could be developed. This proposal created a great deal of apprehension and resistance on the part of executives from several of the divisions. To encourage support, an extensive corporate staff was created where only research and financial groups had previously been in evidence. Many "promotions" to headquarters mollified much of the criticism. This enlarged staff group prospered and grew to substantial size. Their purposes were not as clear as their growth. Vice-presidents in many functions were in evidence. This structure remained in place until the company experienced substantial deficits as a result of the loss of a key customer. At that time, a wholesale housecleaning at headquarters staff occurred, dropping their numbers from 1,900 to 300 within a six-month period.

Thus far, little has been explicitly discussed about the political activities that are directed toward personal goals or special interests rather than toward task performance and overall organizational goals. Even while carrying undesirable connotations, political activities can further overall objectives. To illustrate, a group of supervisors, dissatisfied with their treatment, pay, and status, attempted to form a supervisory union in one company. This effort raised the question of why organizing activities were being undertaken. The underlying causes of dissatisfaction were identified and corrected, so that the bargaining effort and the reason for it disappeared.

Much political action of organizational participants is directed toward the narrow goals of their subunit or toward their personal goals and interests. To the extent that political behaviors are widespread in an organization, the numerous goals pursued are inconsistent with overall goals. A politicized organization can create many small coalitions, none of which have sufficient power to dominate the affairs of the firm to lead it in a consistent direction.

STRATEGY AND COALITIONS

The strategy of a firm can influence which individuals and coalitions are powerful in an organization. Firms that are evolutionary in character continuously develop new products as a means of competing in their environments. Hewlett Packard and 3M are examples of firms that put a lot of emphasis upon and reward for new product development. In such evolutionary firms, in general, the most powerful members are those most closely associated with the activity that enhances the values for developing new products or services. Those individuals associated with the research, marketing, and engineering functions of the firm are those involved with the initial birth and introduction of new products. Since these activities are more highly regarded in such a firm, those individuals within those functions possess higher power, and coalitions of them are able to dictate much of what the future of the firm is likely to be.

It ought to be recognized that there is a danger of circular reasoning in such an explanation. The reason that product or service development is prized in the first place is the implanting of these values as important sometime in the past. Such philosophical expectations and values were often developed by the founder of the firm or by some powerful dominant manager. Thus, past powerful individuals or coalitions furthered these values in the first place. These preferred values then provide the basis of subsequent power to those coalitions or individuals who best represent the furtherance of them.

In contrast with evolutionary firms are those that excel in efficiency and stability. Such firms do not change their market product strategies frequently, but they do attempt to optimize those products they have in the markets they service. Rather than use intense pressure to develop new products, such firms seek to excel in producing what they do have better and more efficiently. Either strategy may be successful for a time. The powerful coalitions in a stable strategy firm tend to be those that focus upon the efficiency of the enterprise. Accountants and financial experts, production managers, and industrial and process engineers tend to represent the types of professionals that possess the expertise to best service the efficiency values held in esteem in firms with stable strategies.

Whether the functional politicized behavior of individuals in firms is valuable or dysfunctional cannot be equivocally answered. Since emphasis upon the functions of marketing and new product development in an evolutionary firm tends to promote those actions that are consistent with achieving its strategies, powerful coalitions within or among the individuals assigned to these functions appear to achieve an intended result. It is only when these powerful members or groups exercise their power for personal or other nonorganizational purposes that the existence of the politicized coalitions associated with the strategy results in dysfunction.

POLITICS, STRATEGY, AND FUTURE DIRECTIONS

Early 1984 saw two instances of political struggles within and a power play from outside the company to restructure the directions of the companies involved. Upon the breakup of AT&T, the communications industry was thrown into a competitive war in which the old Bell systems were going to have to compete much more vigorously than previously required in the protected regulated environment of a monopoly. Under these circumstances, AT&T hired a number of marketing experts to plan and execute the strategies that the firm was expecting to use in its new unregulated role. The newcomers to AT&T were soon locked in a power struggle with old-time production executives from Western Electric. As the production executives gained ascendancy, a number of marketing executives, recruited from powerful consumer product firms, started to leave. The power of the past appeared dominant, even in the light of new market demands.

The power of old coalitions in U.S. Steel also seemed alive and well if the decision to try to acquire National Steel is any indication. For some prior period of time, U.S. Steel had been embarking on a diversification strategy into chemicals and oil while closing down a number of outmoded steel facilities. The choice to return to a more intensive stance in the steel business was seen as a victory for the steel people in the company, even though the competitiveness of the steel industry in light of foreign competition was open to serious question. Again, the old power of coalitions within a company had returned a company in the directions from which it had come—away from the new diversification moves it had made. The acquisition decision was called off because of the inability to gain Justice Department approval, rather than from a definitive decision about the proper direction of the firm.

In contrast with the situations of old coalitions returning an organization to its former directions, the plans of Mesa Petroleum's chairman, T. Boone Pickens, Jr., included acquiring Gulf Oil for the purported purpose of breaking the firm into parts (rather than keeping it integrated) so that greater values could be created for Gulf's stockholders (including Pickens). Mesa's actions ultimately forced Gulf to seek a white knight to acquire it. Its resources were undervalued by the market, a fact recognized by Pickens in his breakup plans. The acquiring firm, Socal, will follow its own strategy in absorbing and deploying the assets of Gulf, but this is unlikely to follow either the Gulf or the Mesa scenarios. If the power of officers in charge of a public firm fails to satisfy shareholders, it raises the opportunity for corporate raiders to develop a competing coalition of investors to seek control and new directions for the firm.

SUMMARY

The logical and rational persons in us seek understanding of an organization by its design and intent. We decry the political battles that attempt to bend the purposes to those preferred by others. Yet, at the same time, we may use our own powers, however limited they may be at times, to push the organization in the direction that we believe it ought to go. To some extent, this jockeying for position by different views of what the organization ought to be can be valuable as a test of what the organization is to become. In a sense, this political activity provides a test of wills between competing ideas to formulate the nature of the organization. Thus, a chief executive may welcome, for a time, this interplay to continue until the various factions within the firm have evolved positions from which may be selected a proper course of direction and action. This could be particularly beneficial when the uncertainty of future directions is in considerable doubt.

The danger of politicizing is that it will be used to further personal interests in opposition to the best interests of the corporation. Separating the effect of political activity of personal from organizational gain is difficult, because the effects that promote organizational gain have, at the same time, an effect upon personal careers of individuals. The role of the chief executive officer is to hold the rational and political perspectives within reasonable balance. The complete reliance on rational methods may fail to allow the interplay of competing ideas. Conversely, unfettered political decision making shoves out any rational and logical organizational purpose, design, or operation. Without insistence that rational planning be carried out as a basis for operations, the CEO runs the risks of commission or omission in considering the future of the enterprise. Competing ideas can be brought to the table for consideration if the CEO provides some sort of forum within the organization where these antagonists' views can be aired and considered. The freedom of expression in decision making, if considered fair and proper by those with diverse views, will counter the tendency of purely political behaviors dominating the affairs of the organization.

4

Setting Economic Goals

The purpose of this chapter is to explain how to establish economic goals at the business and corporate levels. To illustrate the techniques that are being suggested, we use the F. W. Woolworth Company as an example throughout a good portion of the analysis.

FIRST STEP: WHAT CAN BE ACCOMPLISHED?

As we indicated in Chapter 1, the content and level of the objectives need to be established as a first approach to setting goals. A tentative answer to the question of what can be accomplished in both content and level of a goal is to look at what other comparable companies are accomplishing. The problem with such a line of inquiry is to answer what is a "comparable" company with which to compare our target business. A first approximation is to identify competitors. The industry in which the firm competes consists of companies with comparable capabilities and able to achieve results similar to our target firm's. The industry classifications are often, however, too broad such that they encompass firms with widely varying customer bases, product offerings, or investment requirements. Porter (1980) recommends that strategic analysis at the four-digit level of the Standard Industrial Classification Code is the proper degree of differentiation and similarity sought, the three-digit level being too broad and the five-digit level being too narrow.

Performance Across Industries

Table 4.1 shows the profitability and growth of a group of industries, selected to illustrate differences in industry performances.

Table 4.1 1982 Profitability and Growth: Selected Industries

	ROI	ROE	Sales Growth
Industry	*1982 (%)*		*1979–82 (%)*
Auto and truck	1.9	0.3	−4.36
Health care—hospital suppliers	15.0	17.5	14.6
Distilling and tobacco	13.0	17.0	9.8
Petroleum, integrated	10.4	12.4	225.4
Rail equipment	5.3	5.4	−9.0
Electrical utility	7.7	11.0	22.9
Toiletries and cosmetics	13.0	5.0	14.4
Household products	15.0	17.2	9.8
Computer services	13.0	15.5	28.9
Metals and mining	0.5	NMF*	5.16
Conglomerate	8.0	10.0	9.7
Sugar	9.5	11.0	13.5
Publishing	13.5	15.5	19.2
Diversified chemicals	9.5	11.5	7.8
Textile	4.5	5.2	4.6

Note: Most financial data for this and other tables in this chapter were derived from *Value Line's Investment Survey* (New York: *Valve Line*, 1983–84).
NMF = Not meaningful

These measures are employed for comparison and analysis because they represent the most frequently used areas within which overall corporate goals are established in American enterprises. From these data, it might appear that it would be profitable to exit the low-return industries by divesting those businesses, using the proceeds to enter the high-profit industries. However, there may be a number of barriers to both exit from an industry and entry to another. Resources are not freely transferable from one industry to another, especially in the short run. In any event, in setting goals for a company, it appears more practical to set them in relation to what can be accomplished within the competitive industry of which the firm is a part, rather than to take an average of all companies in all industries or of the best firms in the economy as a whole. It should be noted in Table 4.1 that the 1979–82 period was one of rapid inflation and declining economic activity, the latter occurring in 1981 and 1982. Comparisons over a longer period of time to smooth irregularities can be even more useful in seeking a basis to establish overall long-term goals for a business.

Performance Within an Industry

Assigning firms to an industry is based primarily upon the similarity of products that the participants manufacture or distribute, or the manner in which their economic function is carried out. These criteria for grouping firms fail to consider all of the competitive factors that influence the ability of the firm to achieve a given level of results. For example, the steel industry is composed of specialty product or process firms as well as the fully integrated broad-line producers. In some markets, the specialty producers do not compete against the integrated full-line companies. The minimills that have proliferated in the industry since 1970 usually have a specialty product (e.g., line pipe), are not integrated in that they utilize scrap reprocessing rather than the basic steel processes, and usually distribute their products in a limited geographical area. If we were to compare the minimills with the full-line producers, the goals that either would be able to achieve typically would be quite different from the other. Similarly, their real competitors may be the Japanese or German steelmakers such that foreign accomplishments and capabilities need to be taken into account in establishing what any firm may reasonably be expected to accomplish. Yet, despite technological and market scope differences, inability of one group of competitors to match achievements of other segments indicates competitive weaknesses, no matter which objectives it sets or how it sets them.

As we seek similarities and differences among firms, we must also recognize that the competitive characteristics of the basic steel industry may have many similarities to those of the basic chemical industry. A method for analyzing such conditions is developed later in this chapter.

In the next section, we illustrate the basic procedures for setting or evaluating economic objectives for a firm, using F. W. Woolworth as an example. We are attempting to evaluate the profit and growth goals that the management of the firm has established. The first task is to identify the firms with which Woolworth is comparable, the industry, the subsets of the industry, and their profitability and growth over several periods of time. Although Woolworth is in the retail store industry, it has several different business units that vary a great deal from each other in terms of profitability and growth. Thus, these factors are analyzed for each of the parts and comparisons made in the light of past performance to arrive at a conglomerate rate of profit and growth that can reasonably be expected. The company has made several changes in strategy that will influence its ability to achieve any set level of goals, and adjustments must be made to determine its capability in light of these factors. Finally, a crude sensitivity analysis is undertaken to accommodate upside potentials and downside risks in achieving the level of objectives that the firm has established.

F. W. Woolworth

The F. W. Woolworth Company is classified by Value Line as a member of the retail store industry. Woolworth has several lines of business within its overall corporate strategy. The largest group consists of the variety stores, which have followed basically the same strategy for most of this century. A second line is the Richman Brothers chain, a men's specialty clothing store. Third are its chains of Kinney Shoe stores, J. Brannam stores, off-price brand name outlets, and Susie Shoe stores. In addition, there are substantial foreign operations in Canada and Europe. In January 1983, the company shut down its Woolco operations and sold its assets. In 1982 it divested its British stores.

The Retail Store Industry. There are thirty-five firms listed by Value Line (1983, 1984) as participating in the retail store industry. Even though Value Line is selective in the firms it reports upon because it is interested in reporting the bulk of public firms on the stock market, the sample can be used to illustrate selecting comparable firms for analysis in setting economic goals.

Table 4.2 makes these comparisons. The industry has grown at a 9.7 percent compound rate from 1978–82, but in real, inflation-adjusted terms, there has probably been a decline. This is in spite of

Table 4.2 Performance Differences: Average, Retail Store Industry Versus Woolworth

Performance Area	Retail Industry*	Woolworth
	1978–82 Compound Rates (%)	
Sales growth	9.7	−4.3
Growth, number of stores	19.5	1.95
Net profit growth	−2.1	−10.9
Growth, net worth	7.9	−4.0
Percentage ROI, 1978	10.4	7.3
1982	9.0	7.1
Percentage ROE, 1978	13.2	11.1
1982	10.9	8.2

*n = 35

the increase in the number of retail outlets that have had an absolute decline in dollar volume per store and a more drastic decline in real inflation-adjusted sales. As relatively more stores are added than population increases, more stores tend to generate greater competitive rivalry among outlets. This is reflected in the industry decline in absolute dollar profit in spite of the growth of facilities. It is emphasized further by the declines in both returns on investment and equity. The industry data confirm a long-term trend for greater rivalry within retailing in the United States.

Woolworth's performance relative to the industry is rather dismal. The decline in absolute dollar volume is, however, not as poor as it looks. The company liquidated the Woolco division because it was losing money, and divested its British outlets to raise cash to pay debts. A smaller and more profitable Woolworth may be more successful than a larger one that included a large loser, Woolco. This brings up again whether Woolworth should be compared with the industry as a whole.

Industry Subgroups. In the retail store industry are such firms as Federated Department Stores, Charm'g Shoppes, and Allied Stores, which are department stores or high-fashion specialty stores with which the Woolworth group is unlikely to compete except at the fringes. It is possible to select eight firms from the thirty-four others in the industry to identify a more comparable environmental or industry group, the performances of which are more likely to match that of Woolworth. Such an environmental group includes Ames, Dollar General, Family Dollar, K-Mart, G. C. Murphy, Wal-Mart, and Zayre. Even these selections have some variation from the Woolworth mix of businesses and show the preferability of selecting comparable organizations at the line of business level rather than at the corporate level if at all possible. It is, however, not always feasible to find directly comparable businesses. Of all the firms in this industry, however, G. C. Murphy Company appears to be following a strategy closest to that of Woolworth. (See Table 4.3 for comparisons.)

To further determine whether Woolworth's past performance represents the level of performance as a goal toward which the company should aspire, the performances of the retail store industry in 1982 and for the highest levels achieved during the last ten years are presented in Table 4.4. These data are shown for both the industry as a whole and for each of the subgroup firms that are most comparable to the strategies that Woolworth is undertaking. The industry data are presented in quartile format while also indicating the high and low levels of performance for subgroup firms in the industry. Woolworth's performances are in the top of the poorest 25 percent of the firms in the retail store industry. Compared with the competi-

Table 4.3 Profitability: Retail Firms Similar to Woolworth

ROI	ROE		ROI	ROE
1982 (%)			*Maximum %, 1973–82*	
12.2	15.6	Ames	14.1	19.8
15.7	17.8	Dollar General	15.7	17.8
19.4	19.4	Family Dollar	30.2	30.2
7.9	10.1	K-Mart	16.5	18.5
7.1	8.8	G. C. Murphy	7.1	8.8
16.8	25.1	Wal-Mart	18.3	25.1
7.1	8.2	Woolworth	9.7	11.4
8.7	11.9	Zayre	8.7	11.9

tive group of firms with which it is most closely aligned, it ranks at or near the bottom and is quite comparable in performance to G. C. Murphy Company, the firm with which it is considered most comparable. In most respects, this past performance has not been very uplifting or inspiring. The only redeeming feature of it is that it is approximately equal to what its nearest competitor has been able to achieve.

Woolworth Goals Versus Industry Performance

Complicating the problems at Woolworth was the 1982 death of the president, Edward F. Gibbons, whose strategic plans for Woolworth, after the decision to get rid of Woolco, were not communicated to the rest of the management. Further, when John W. Lynn, whose

Table 4.4 Profitability: Retail Store Industry

ROI	ROE		ROI	ROE
1982 (%)			*Highest %, 1973–82*	
20.1	27.4	Highest	39.9	42.5
14.4	15.6	Third quartile	16.5	25.1
9.1	11.9	Median	12.7	15.6
7.4	8.8	First quartile	9.7	11.8
NMF*	NMF	Lowest	5.5	7.5

*NMF = Not meaningful

experience had been with the original variety chain, was named chairman and CEO, a number of younger managers, who saw this appointment as a signal for continuation of the old strategies, resigned from the firm.

Lynn and the new president, Howard E. Sells, have been attempting to wrestle with the problems of the company. They have established several economic goals toward which the firm is to work:

16%	return on equity
11%	return on investment
5%	inflation-adjusted real sales growth
10%	profit growth as a minimum

These goals may be compared with performance of Woolworth and the industry in the past:

	ROI (%)	ROE (%)	Sales Growth 1978–82 (%)	Profit Growth 1978–82 (%)
Woolworth goal, 1983	11	16	5	10.0/yr
Woolworth results, 1978	7.3	11.1	−4.0	−10.9
Industry results, 1978	10.4	13.2	9.7	−2.1

The ROI goal is 50 percent higher for the future than Woolworth was able to achieve with the Woolco operation in place in 1978. The ROE goal is 44 percent higher than the firm's 1978 experience, and performance since that time has declined on both measures through 1982. In addition, both of these goals exceed what the industry was able to achieve on average from 1978–82. The objective for rate of sales growth of 5 percent exceeds that of the industry for the 1978–82 period during which the unadjusted rate was 9.7 percent, during an inflationary period. In spite of the increase in dollar sales, the net profit for the industry declined for the period, while the Woolworth goal is to increase profits 10 percent per year. Comparing these data with those in Table 4.4, it appears that the new management is establishing Woolworth's goals comparable to firms in the most profitable quartile of firms in the industry, but their experience has been in the bottom quartile. We must conclude that these goals are rather ambitious; certainly the levels of these goals meet one of the criteria of a good goal. They are challenging.

Strategy Changes and Profit Possibilities. One of the questions, however, is whether the level of these goals is achievable if Woolworth undertakes a change in its strategy. By 1983, the company had made strategic changes by dropping its Woolco and British operations. Can the elimination of the losses from Woolco and the debt repayments from the proceeds of the British sale allow the firm to meet its financial goals? The answer depends first upon the differences in the margins Woolworth will be able to achieve.

Excluding Woolco and the British operations in 1982, the firm would have earned 5 percent pretax on sales (approximately 3 percent after tax). This compares with the 1.6 percent after taxes they actually achieved with Woolco operating all year and the British operations contributing part of the year. If we restate the 1982 results, the strategic changes bring in an 88 percent increase in after-tax margin. If applied to profit rates earned in the past, estimates of potential returns (given the 5 percent pretax margins could be maintained) would be:

	Income Tax Rate Projections		
	40%	*45%*	*Goal*
ROI	13.7%	10.3%	11.0%
ROE	20.8%	15.6%	16.0%

Woolworth's tax rate has ranged from over 45 percent to as low as 21 percent over the 1978–82 period, but is likely to remain at least 45 percent considering both U.S. and foreign taxes. Thus, it appears that Woolworth's profitability goals set by management in 1983 could be achieved with the 1983 strategy and some moderate changes in operating efficiency. This estimate also takes into account the lesser interests costs to be incurred because of the debt repayments funded from the sale of the British stores.

Strategy and Growth Possibilities. Achieving the growth goals depend upon increasing sales and then increasing profits faster than sales increase. To make an estimate of what can be achieved, it is useful to estimate for each line of business for 1978, as is done for Woolworth in Table 4.5. The strategy of the variety stores is one hundred years old, and little real growth can be expected without substantial strategic marketing changes and investment in store renewal. Given the large debt, it is unlikely that the variety stores will be the target of such changes by Woolworth in the near future. The growth and margin estimates are probably optimistic for this division.

Both Kinney and Richman have been growing at negative real rates (adjusted for inflation). Yet, Kinney has consistently had the

Table 4.5 Estimated Sales and Profits: Woolworth, 1987

	Variety	Kinney	Richman	Brannam	Foreign	Total
1982 sales (million)	$1,707	$910	$198	$85	$2,224	$5,124
1982 profit rate	3.9%	9.7%	2.0%	−5.9%	4.7%	5.0%
Estimated real rates of growth	0%	−2%	−5.0%	25.0%	0%	0.16%
1987 sales (million)	$1,707	$822.6	$153.2	$259.4	$2,224	$5,166.28
Profit rate	3.9%	9.7%	2.0%	5.0%	4.7%	5.2%
1987 profits, b.t.	$ 66.57	$ 79.79	$30.6	$13.0	$ 104.53	$ 267.0

Restated 1982 profits: $256.20 million, b.t.

Estimated profit increase 1982–87: 0.83% per year vs. 10.0%, goal

Estimated sales increase 1982–87: 0.16% per year vs. 5.0%, goal

highest margins of any Woolworth division and has bested a close competitor's margins (Gallenkamp) by 60 percent. Richman's low 2 percent margins in 1982 reflect an improvement from deficit returns in 1980 and 1981. Yet, these esimates may be slightly pessimistic.

While the ability of Woolworth to achieve 1987 goals is dependent upon achieving projections noted in Table 4.5, their dependence upon the Brannam discount chain is critical, since it is the only division expected to earn higher profits in 1987 than in 1982. The past growth of Brannam of 75 percent per year was from a small base. Seventy-five percent growth has a small probability of continuing for another five years because, in comparison, Wal-Mart, one of retailing's most successful firms in the last ten years, grew at a 39.1 percent compound rate. Further, the successful close competitors to Brannam's of Allied and Dayton-Hudson, and others such as Marshall's and Loehman's, have outraced Brannam in the past in terms of growth and profitability. Dayton-Hudson's Mervyn's stores netted 9.9 percent return on sales in 1982 and are enjoying a 27 percent growth rate. Their Target stores are growing at a 25 percent rate while contributing a 4.7 percent profit rate. Since Brannam has lagged behind its competitors in advancing into the name brand discount markets, it is optimistic (and may be gratuitous) to estimate a five-year growth rate of 25 percent per year and a 5 percent net profit in 1987.

Woolworth's foreign operations have been stagnant in terms of recent growth, and margins are declining. We use the 1982 profits and sales as the 1987 estimates.

The total estimated sales for 1987 add to $5,166.2 billion, only a .16 percent compound increase per year versus the goal of 5 percent per year. Similarly, the profit increase amounts to only .83 percent per year versus the 10 percent per year goal. This is not very encouraging. It appears that Woolworth's stated growth goals are going to be much harder to achieve than its profitability goals.

Sensitivity Analysis. The estimates in Table 4.5 are single-value estimates for sales and profits by business divisions within Woolworth. The estimate of real rates of growth for the Kinney division, for example, could be lower or higher than the estimates shown. To deal with the improbability of single-value estimates in an array such as Table 4.5, we can provide different rates of growth and profit rate on sales estimates for a series of estimated sales, profits, and growth thereof. Table 4.6 shows three levels of sales and margins that the Kinney division might experience over the next five years. With proper computer models of any unit's performance being estimated, this type of varying profitability projection is relatively easy compared with hand-calculated analysis. For example, a computer spreadsheet program allows relatively rapid testing of different assumptions and esimtates.

Frequently managers want to know the best and worst case estimates as well as some average value in between. These may be juggled in a large number of combinations and permutations. By estimating three values for two variables for Kinney in Table 4.6, for example, we get the nine estimates of profitability. Figuring that each of the other five divisions of the firm require the same sort of sensitivity analysis, we come up with a large number of combinations to make judgments about. If we seek conservative estimates or optimistic ones only, it does not turn out to be quite as complicated.

Table 4.6 1987 Pretax Profits (Million): Kinney Division Under Different Growth and Margin Conditions

Assumed Rates of Growth Per Year (%)	Assumed Margins, Before Tax		
	13%	*9%*	*4%*
10	$337.4	$247.4	$110.0
0	$221.9	$153.6	$ 68.3
−10	$131.04	$ 90.7	$ 40.3

Note: Actual profit rate in 1982 was 9.7%.

Values and Expectations: Setting Goal Levels

The *estimated* values or combinations at which one is able to arrive are not necessarily as important as are the expectations and values of the managers of the units involved as well as those of top management. These two groups will at some time need to agree on what is expected rather than on merely what can be achieved. If a relatively optimistic and difficult scenario of events is selected, the results for Woolworth might turn out somewhat like the estimates made for Table 4.7:

- The variety stores will do well to maintain an even level of sales and to increase their pretax margins to 5 percent.
- The Table 4.5 estimates for Kinney are not very motivating or uplifting as objectives toward which the division should aspire during the next five years, so the levels have been increased.
- A similar line of reasoning prevails for the Richman chain's objective, although Richman management will need to refashion much of what they have been doing in the past in order to grow.
- The Brannam estimates in Table 4.5 were carried over to Table 4.7 because they represent rather good performances relative to the industry and what has gone on previously within Woolworth.
- If the economy in Europe recovers as expected, a 5 percent increase in sales and a modest increase in margins might well provide a challenging and achievable goal for these operations.

The result of these goals, if achieved, would be a profit increase of 15.9 percent per year and a sales growth of 9 percent for Woolworth as a whole. These far exceed the goals that the management has

Table 4.7 1987 Divisional-Corporate Profit and Growth Goals With 1983 Strategy: Woolworth, Favorable Scenario

	Variety	Kinney	Richman	Brannam	Foreign	Total
Sales goal (%)	0	10	10	25	10	11.0
Profit rate goal (%)	5	10	5	7.5	6	7.1
1987 sales goal (million)	$1,707	$2,749	$318	$259	$2,838	$7,871
1987 profits (million)	$ 85.4	$ 275	$ 16	$ 19.5	$ 170.3	$ 536

Profit increase per year: 15.9%

Sales increase per year: 9.0%

Return on sales, 1987: 6.8%

established. What these margins and growth rates would generate in terms of ROI or ROE would depend upon how much extra investment would be required to generate this growth. Since we have used real (equivalent to physical volume) growth, it is likely that additional investments will be required for at least the Kinney, Richman, and Brannam businesses. Furthermore, investments for growth in one type of business can be considerably different than that for another one. The inventory turnover in shoe stores, for example is approximately one-half what it is for soft goods. As a consequence, the investments required in Kinney to increase volume as set forth in Table 4.7 would be greater per dollar of volume increase than they would for the Richman or Brannam chains. Without getting into considerable detail and beyond the author's knowledge, it is not feasible to develop specific investment estimates for Woolworth here. It should be noted that Kinney's goal for increasing sales 10 percent per year could be accomplished with less investment increase if the emphasis were upon increasing sales per store rather than getting the increased volume from new stores. Such alternatives would need to be taken into consideration in setting overall ROI and ROE objectives for each particular business and then for the organization as a whole.

RECAPITULATION

To summarize the process of setting economic goals through comparable companies in the industry, the following steps should be noted.

1. Identify the industry or industries within which the company or the business divisions of the company compete.
2. Identify the companies or the divisions of other companies who are most directly the competitors of the firm or its subdivisions or both.
3. Determine the performance characteristics and growth measures that are to be used in setting objectives.
4. Calculate a range of values of the competitive business's performance or growth measures that are to be compared.
5. Estimate the future values of the measures of performance or growth (or both) that you are employing as objectives for the businesses and company for which objectives are being established.
6. Develop a sensitivity analysis of the values for the measures noted in 5 above.

7. Make a judgment about whether some mix of the sensitivity analysis estimates provides a satisfactory matrix of goals for each of the businesses and for the enterprise as a whole.
8. Adjust the estimates to align them with the expectations of the managers and their aspirations of the firm.

One may question why one would go through such a long and drawn-out process if on the basis of judgment, personal values, and aspirations, the goals are going to be changed anyway. Why not start with the end of the process and be done with it? The answer lies in the information that the process provides to inform the managers who are involved with developing and achieving the goals. Without the process, knowledge about what the industry will ordinarily allow to be achieved, given its competitive climate and so forth, brings one up short in merely selecting goals by the seat of the pants.

Beyond Analysis

Setting corporate-level goals is not merely a question of adding up the goals of each of the divisions of the corporation to arrive at an overall objective. While such an exercise provides a level of corporate goal that will be achieved, given that each of the divisions arrives at the objectives that it sets, this effort may be insufficient. If the corporate management provides no more than the sum of the divisions as what the total organization is to strive for, it acts as little more than a bargaining agent with the heads of the business divisions. A top management who expects excellence ought to insist upon such a guiding philosophy being reflected in corporate, divisional, and functional goals throughout the organization. For such reason, top management ordinarily will not merely accept the summation of independently arrived at lower-level objectives as the corporate objectives.

The corporate objectives rather should reflect the visions and values of the best conceptual thought of its top leadership. It is this special role in which the highest levels of leadership should and often do excel. Corporate managers will have their own independent visions of what the corporation ought to achieve, no matter what the divisions come up with. It is one of the functions of corporate objectives to inform and drive the corporate strategy of the firm. If any division of the firm, either strategically or operationally, is unable to contribute to corporation aspirations, the strategy question for the top leadership is whether the divisions performing poorly with respect to corporate goals should remain as part of the corporate mix of businesses in which the enterprise is to participate. Inability to consistently meet or move toward the accomplishment of corporate objectives is a trigger to consider restructuring the strategy of the less than satisfactory unit, divesting the unit, or bringing in a new management of the division to restructure it toward corporate goals.

In the situation facing Woolworth, many external analysts question whether the top leadership has been convincing in setting viable approaches to achieving their profit and growth objectives. They see little growth for the variety stores and a fumbling with Brannam's strategic stance or operational activities or both. Further, some observers question whether the concept of Richman as a retail entity can survive in present competitive markets. After all, Richman has not been a significant contributor to corporate objectives for some time. The objectives established for both Brannam and Richman in Tables 4.5 and 4.7 are rather ambitious in the light of their past performances. What is it that would allow these operations to turn around to such an extent that the goals could reasonably be expected to be achieved?

It may be possible, in the light of the improbability that the goals have much chance of success, to sell these divisions to other firms with whom they might be able to achieve a degree of success. This change in strategy for Woolworth may not be very practical, however, if the buyers for the divisions cannot be found or if the prices that can be received for the divisions are so small that the current returns on divestment proceeds would meet current corporate goals. If the latter is the case, the value of these operations may merely be overpriced on the balance sheet.

It is in this manner that corporate goals influence strategy to restructure the strategies at divisional levels or drive corporate management to change the strategic mix of businesses in which the firm is to operate.

IS INDUSTRY THE RIGHT SURROGATE FOR ENVIRONMENT?

In the above analysis, we first identified the industry in which the firm for which we are setting goals is operating, and then selected a smaller subset of firms within that industry that appeared to undertake similar activities. This process was intended to develop a set of companies or businesses within companies that were comparable to those of the target firm. This procedure is similar to that recommended by Porter (1980). There is considerable debate, however, whether this procedure is necessary or desirable. We suggested in our initial analysis that the basic chemical industry might exhibit some of the same competitive characteristics that the basic steel industry does. If so, the actions taken by basic steel producers might have results similar to firms who follow the same type of actions in the basic chemical industry. This idea is behind the development of the PIMS data base. The original conception of this data base at General Electric was based on the search for common factors for successful and unsuccessful businesses within General Electric and its competitors. A number of factors were identified. These can be classed into two groups: environmental factors and company conduct variables. The PIMS data base is a generalization of that idea to a large number of participating businesses. PIMS solicits data at the business level from a number of different companies. Studies have been made (and continue) to identify degrees of business success (and the lack of it) under different environmental and operating conditions. Thus, the PIMS environmental data can supplant the industry idea; one is able to identify a number of environmental factors and the degree to which they have an effect upon profitability, growth, or other result-oriented factors. Similarly, a number of strategic factors are available for analysis in the same way. Sid Schoeffler, head of the PIMS project, has stated that industry does not make a difference in results across firms;[1] rather it is the distinctive intersection of environmental-strategic conditions that determines success or failure. This is important to the goal-setting process, because PIMS can immediately provide a set of comparable businesses that face the same competitive conditions. Further, the PIMS service to corporations (available for a fee for participants) is able to identify strategic and operating changes that a business can undertake to improve its results.

These analyses from PIMS could be of considerable value in establishing the goals and strategies that potentially could improve the performance of the business and the whole corporation of which it is a part. These data are also available without company identification to qualified researchers, as the following example illustrates.

Environmental Groups

By statistical clustering of the environmental factors associated with each of the firms in the PIMS data base, adjusted for software limits,

1. The contention that industry does not matter may be biased, since PIMS has too small a sample to provide enough statistical data in a large number of industries.

Prescott (1983) was able to identify eight separate competitive environments, each of which included companies from a number of different industries. Each of these firms, in any one environment, however, was facing similar competitive factors as well as degrees of similar environmental press or opportunity. As a substitute for industry as the external forces that a company may face, the competitive environments (as has been previously noted) provide a specification of the competitive factors with which the firm deals.

Strategic Groups

Prescott also developed strategic groups within each of the competitive environments. Each of the strategic groups undertook different strategies or patterns for allocating its resources as its distinctive approach to the market. Further, the differences in performances suggested the relative superiority or inferiority of alternate strategies.

Table 4.8 reports a portion of the results of Prescott's study. There were only two environments of the eight that provided statistically superior or inferior results: The global importing environment was superior to all other environments, and the fragmented standard products environment had below-average performance. Similarly, within each of the environments, there were differences in the performance turned in by each of the different strategies employed there.[2] Across all environments, the strategy of market domination was the most profitable. Yet, the low-cost strategy was able to achieve a 46.34 percent ROI in the declining competitive environment, a combination of environment and strategy that had the highest return of any in the Prescott study.

Performance

The effects of environment, however, were not as great as the impact of the strategy used in the environment. Prescott reports that the strategic influences had twelve times more importance in explaining a firm's performance than did the environmental forces. A dominance of strategy over environment can also be estimated by examining the range of ROIs in Table 4.1 with those reported in Table 4.3. The variation of performance of the several strategies reported in Table 4.3 is greater than the differences across industries reported

2. It should be noted that the strategies shown in Table 4.8 are generic strategies developed across all firms, rather than the more specific strategic groups developed within each different environment.

Table 4.8 Return on Investment (%) by Selected Environments and Strategies

	Basic Strategies					
Environments	*Environmental Mean*	*High Market Share*	*Follow Leaders*	*Prestige Approach*	*Low Cost*	*Low Quality*
Global importing	28.63*	42.43†	28.93			19.12† 31.17
Declining	20.37	43.47†	26.11	20.80	46.34†	15.41 14.47
Fragmented standard products	14.51*		20.71 27.91	9.45		9.07 15.60 11.24
All	21.88	42.06†	32.95	30.83	29.31	18.65

Source: Prescott (1983).

Notes: Some basic strategies were not employed in some of the environments (e.g., low-cost strategy in the global importing environment). Variations of basic strategies were used in some environments (e.g., two low-quality approaches in the declining environment).

*Significantly different from all environments

†Significantly different from the mean of the strategies used in that environment

in Table 4.1. This finding is important in deciding what to do if a business fails to meet its goals. While the common wisdom in this event is to consider changing corporate strategy by disinvesting the business, the data suggest that greater performance improvement might well result instead from changing the strategy at the business level. Which approach is preferred in any situation would depend upon the costs of each approach compared with its benefits.

Even if the decision is to divest a division of the firm so that the proceeds can be reinvested in another line of business, it may be worthwhile to change the strategy of the division prior to divesting it in order to increase its returns so as to improve its attractiveness to potential buyers of the business. As Table 4.8 shows, if the firm was operating in the declining environment and carrying out a low-quality strategy, increases in ROI could be expected, on the average, if it were to shift its strategy to any of the others, but particularly to the low-cost strategy.

The use of an environmental-strategic approach to assaying strategic objectives is not limited to the use of the PIMS data base. Corporate data are available from *Moody's, Standard and Poor's, Value Line, Forbes, Fortune,* and similar sources. The problem with most of these sources is that they do not provide multiple measures of environmental data on an objective and consistent basis, although some may be calculated from other data available. PIMS measures these factors directly in multiple dimensions—a considerable advantage. The data are available via electronic communication means for rapid access. Such advantages cannot be claimed for most of the other data sources. Census data may be an exception. The widespread use of PIMS-like data may await the development of an information utility incorporating strategic and environmental information.

We have noted the advantage of the nonindustry formats of competitive analysis of performance as being the ability to identify the specific environmental factors that are influencing competition for a firm. It may well be, however, that considerable experience in an industry will allow a firm to identify these factors or absence of them in its industry. Yet, the relative strength of these factors would be more difficult to figure, because less intercompany comparisons could be made. PIMS itself has less difficulty in this regard because it has a relatively large, even though not random, sample of respondents.

USING ENVIRONMENTAL AND STRATEGIC GROUPS IN GOAL SETTING

The problem that any business has in utilizing the approach of going beyond industry to identify comparable firms is the uncertainty of classifying their own firm to a specific environmental group and to a generic or specific strategy within that group without becoming a member of the PIMS program at a considerable cost per year. It may well be worth the cost to give assurance that one's objectives are being established with the greatest degree of available information. Many other advantages accrue as well. As a shortcut, a firm may be able to determine the environmental group in which the firm resides and the generic or specific within environmental strategy that most closely resembles its own. Employing studies such as Prescott's would make it possible to identify the average and standard deviations of returns that comparable firms have generated in the time frames studied in these reports. These data would indicate the range of reasonable goals to set. Further, this method may be superior to utilizing an industry approach. Too often, an industry consists of unlike aggregates of firms that make within-industry comparisons less than fully useful.

On the other hand, employing comparisons against firms not in the same industry means that the firm is comparing itself to firms with similar conditions facing them and (going further) with strategies similar to its own. However, these firms are, for the most part, not the firm's competitors, except in the resource markets.

SUMMARY

This chapter has been concerned with the process of setting economic objectives at the business and corporate levels of the firm. Neither corporate objectives nor business-level goals can be established in isolation from each other nor from the competitive environments within which they operate. If corporate goals are established without consideration of what can be accomplished, the resulting objectives may well vary quite a bit from reality, either too high or too low. At the business level, if goals are set without reference to what competitive firms with similar or alternate strategies are able to achieve, a practical goal is not likely to emerge from whatever process of goal setting is used. In a similar way, if the goal-setting process at the business level fails to consider what corporate leaders believe the organization should aspire to, the acceptance of the business objectives established in that isolation will require extraordinary negotiations and probable change before resolution. Thus, while there are considerable objective comparisons that can be made as a basis for generating goals, there is coincidently a great deal of messaging of these data, compromise, and trade-offs to be considered. In reality, there is no cookbook approach that can slavishly be followed to arrive at a definitive result. As one can imagine, there can be (and tends to be) politicking, jockeying for position, and a lot of superfluous communication inherent in the interpersonal processes. These process questions are examined in more detail in Chapter 6, but first, Chapter 5 examines setting noneconomic objectives.

5

Considering Social Goals

Economic goals are most important for a business firm. Economic objectives coalesce much analysis and planning that reflect personal aspirations, possibilities in the market, probable competitive moves, and estimates of the firm's abilities in the future. In addition to the factors we considered in Chapter 3, are the environmental and social factors that the firm may wish to (or may be forced to) consider in its planning.

It should be recognized that accommodating external demands alters the firm's goal structure. Either more goals or constraints are attended to, or some of the goals sought rationally may need to be lowered (or even eliminated) so that resources can be devoted to fulfilling new expected results. This chapter first examines organizations as open systems adapting to environments. An examination of social and environmental changes is followed by framing the analysis in terms of social responsibility. A final section then reframes corporate social responsibility in terms similar to those of the start of the discussion, namely, organizations as open systems adapting to their environments.

ORGANIZATIONS AS ADAPTING SYSTEMS

Hospitals, universities, business firms, and other organizations can be better understood if considered as continually interacting with their customers, suppliers, and the social, technological, legal, and political environments within which they operate. If the behavior of these external environments and institutions is stable, placid, and predictable, an organization can focus its operations upon maintaining that external stability while increasing internal efficiency. The firm following a steady-state strategy seeks out a market and product combination that is stable and large enough that its efficiency can be attained and maintained.

Variations in the environmental factors influential to the operation of the firm may be predictable (for example, seasonal sales variation) and taken into account. Consider the effect that seasonal sales have upon the system. Choices need to be made between the costs of carrying inventories, if a steady production rate is sought throughout the year, versus the costs of getting resources to meet production requirements during the peak sales months. Note that predicting the extent and timing of the external variation in sales is required if the system is to adapt successfully. The sales forecasting then needs to be coupled with cost and profit analyses of the impact of the two alternatives (varying production or inventories) as means for adapting.

But more than the net effects upon profit is involved, for variation in rates of production also results in variation in the rate of employment and paychecks of employees. Whatever hardship is endured by employees is an important social factor. The most profitable alternative may not be selected. During the 1981–83 recession, an owner of a small trucking firm remarked that he was running four more rigs than necessary to "take care of" four employees. His running fleet consisted of only fifteen trucks at that time. Yet, he remarked that "we are luckier than most firms." He believed that maintaining employment for four more employees was more important than the substantial costs his firm was incurring.

Additional organizational *differentiation* through adding the functions of forecasting and means of adapting is also required. Then, organizational *integration* to couple these two functions is required as a result of the environmental variation. Galbraith and Kazanjian (1986) provide an exhaustive analysis of differentiation of organization structures and processes together with the several means of integrating the resulting greater complexity of organizational functioning.

That some environments are more dynamic is illustrated by the differences in the technological changes in steel versus chemical firms. Steel firms spend slightly more than 1 percent of sales volume for research and development. Chemicals have a much more rapid rate of technological change to cope with, expending 3 to 5 percent of sales on R&D. The relative size of product research and engineering groups in chemical firms is much greater than in steel firms. Strategy by selecting the kind of domains within which the firm operates can increase or reduce the amount of environmental variation with which the organization must deal. Aggressive firms seek (and attempt to create) changes in the environment with which their flexible technology and skills can deal. Steady-state firms seek to avoid uncertainty.

Just as market or technological changes create the need for internal adjustment, so do social, legal, and political changes. When the Joint Commission on Accrediting Hospitals seeks to implement increased safety from staph infections, individual hospitals may be required to alter their procedures, develop a task force organization to develop adequate procedures, and so on. Laws banning discrimination in employment have given rise to new positions in the personnel departments of universities, banks, and other firms.

Not all external changes are predictable. The Arab oil embargo was generally unexpected. Its impact upon auto, high-use energy industries, homes, and the government has been substantial, and the whole country incurs costs in attempting to adapt to the changes implicit in OPEC functioning. Even steady-state organizations were not able to avoid the effects of the embargo. Because aggressive firms deal with market and technological uncertainties on a regular basis, one might expect them to deal with social or political changes better than those who do not. Bowman and Haire (1975) found high profitability to be associated with high social responsibility in food-processing firms. They hypothesized that *both* were effects from a high capacity for environmental adaptation.

HISTORICAL PERSPECTIVES

The political, legal, and economic environments within which U.S. firms operate have varied over the years. The U. S. political system was founded upon the principles of individual freedom and equality through democratic representative forms of political institutions. This freedom was extended to the means of production and distribution in the form of a free capitalistic enterprise system. At the beginning, laws and regulatory activities were directed at encouraging the development of manufactures and foreign trade. Encouragements were many and limitations were few. Mee (1963) contends that the ethical, religious, and social climate complemented legal and politician individualism. Economic and social progress flourished; the factory system displaced the craft systems predominant in colonial periods.

As markets expanded in the United States and as new technologies became available, large-scale enterprise came into being. Swift saw the potential in the refrigerated railroad car for concentrating slaughter, cutting, and distribution of meat to eliminate the inefficiencies of local butchering. Chandler (1977) shows that many inventive technologies were developed during the decade of the 1880s that allowed efficiency through large-scale enterprise. The pattern was repeated in shoe machinery, sewing machines, oil, tobacco, and other industries, but where technology did not develop (for example, dressmaking) to make large scale economically attractive, small-scale firms remain to this day.

The attractiveness of large-scale enterprise supported by markets sufficiently large to justify investments in the mass technologies led such firms to domination and control of markets and prices. Monopoly profits existed at the expense of most members of society, so that antitrust and antimonopoly laws were ultimately instituted to remedy perceived inequities. Similarly, the deleterious impact of employing child labor was recognized, and laws regulating such employment basically eliminated the practice. These events obviously changed the economic rules of the game under which organizations had been operating. From virtual complete freedom and encouragement to operate in whatever manner businesses saw fit, business activity was undergoing a change brought about by constraint and prohibition of certain behaviors.

In the more recent era, the managements of many firms perceive their environments as unfriendly rather than as encouraging. The regulation of the issuance and sale of securities, the requirement to report profits by line of products, product warranty requirements, personnel hiring, promotion and dismissal rules and regulations, requirements to comply with the Occupational Safety and Health Act (OSHA), limits to information from executives during collective bargaining, pollution requirements, and so forth, combine to give the impression to managers that external environments influencing internal operations are changing more rapidly and imposing more constraints. Executives question whether the free enterprise system can survive under the burden of what many perceive as excessive regulation. Over the long term, institutions of most kinds have been increasingly constrained in the United States. Since, as shown in Chapter 1, the difference between a goal and a constraint is more a matter of degree than of kind, organizations are required to allocate resources in order to achieve both goals and constraints. The 1980–84 efforts at deregulation have reduced governmental constraints while adding competitive factors to consider.

Jacoby (1971) contends that the economic system is formulated, encouraged, and constrained by the political system. Changes in societal values are reflected more or less perfectly in the laws and regulations formed by political systems to control the behavior of the economic system.

→ Individuals → values held → political system → economic system ┐

As values of individuals are altered, they may influence the economic system directly, as exemplified by the inability of General Public Utilities to reopen the undamaged nuclear reactor at Three Mile Island. In the case of air pollution, conversely, American automobile firms did little to reduce emissions until forced to do so by California and federal legislation. Thus, Jacoby contends that it is the role of the political system to establish the conditions under which the economic system is to operate. The role of the economic system within the social and political environment is to supply the goods and services desired by society.

From the viewpoint of society as a whole, the continual imposition of additional constraints upon business firms (and other organizations) has its social costs. For example, requiring the use of lead-free gasoline in automobiles reduces air pollution. At the same time, it raises the costs of gasoline and reduces the miles per gallon that otherwise could be achieved with leaded gas. The Reagan administration's deregulation efforts manifest the belief that constraining business has gone too far. If overcontrol or excess regulation occurs, American firms are disadvantaged compared with foreign competitors that do not incur expenses resulting from "excess" control.

From the view of a firm, deregulation is usually welcomed, but if removal of artificial barriers upon business behavior opens the organization to increased competition (especially from overseas), the firm or the industry of which it is a part may seek other restrictive rules. Import quotas have been sought by the auto and steel industries. Furthermore, governmental loans or bailouts have been sought by aerospace, automobile, and farming interests. Thus, since 1980 there has been a philosophical change at the federal level in the United States. The prior reliance upon government planning as a means of controlling firm behavior has gradually been de-emphasized to allow competitive responses to exert greater and greater control over actions of individual firms. In some cases, decontrol is welcomed as paperwork and restrictions are reduced; in other cases, decontrol lays bare the noncompetitive dependencies that the firm (or industry) has relied upon.

CHANGING SOCIAL VALUES

Important recent shifts have occurred in the values held by American society. Since these value changes are widespread and quite different from those held twenty-five years ago, their changing impact upon business and other kinds of organizations has not had time to be felt completely. Yet, these changes can have profound influence upon the goals sought by organizations together with their modes of operation.

The manifestations of these value changes was not so evident until articulated by the student movements in the mid-1960s, although the students were merely coalescing value changes that had imperceptibly been occurring in the population as a whole (Yankelovich 1977). Additionally, the radicalization of the student movement stemmed from the Vietnam War. When that war ended, radicalization stopped, but the value changes remained. Yankelovich's research indicates a diffusion of these values throughout the U. S. population such that student values no longer vary a great deal from those of the general populace.

Yankelovich identifies the following recent transformations in values.

1. *Hard work.* Significantly less people believe that it pays off or is worth the "nose to the grindstone" efforts to achieve success.
2. *Authority and restraint.* There is a desire for release from constraints of the boss, disagreement with laws, drug use, marriage role, family, religion, manners, morals, and patriotism.
3. *Morality.* New attitudes and freedom toward sex, rationale for war, kinds of friendships, interpersonal relations, and attitudes toward property.
4. *Self-fulfillment.* A desire for self-gratification; less emphasis upon sacrifice and role obligations.
5. *Entitlement.* Individuals have basic rights to food, shelter, health, and education.
6. *Naturalness.* Harmony with nature. Being at one with nature versus strife.

Rather than representing a return to values previously held, these changes, according to Yankelovich, are permanent, still-evolving attitudinal changes.

Influences of Value Changes

The impact of these value changes has already been substantial. These influences include the creation of substantial markets for back-to-nature products (for example, diet, health products, camping), growing concern for the environment, proposals for universal health care, guaranteed annual wage, antiwar demonstrations, sexual freedom, acceptance of unmarrieds living together, women's liberation, antidiscrimination regulations, and worker participation.

Lodge (1974, 64) shows some basic business implications consistent with and echoed by the Yankelovich findings. "Individual fulfillment for most depends upon a place in the community, an identity with the whole, a participation in an organic social process." This carries the concept of individualism to a point that the person has a right to self-fulfillment within a social (and organizational) context. Entitlement erodes the concept of private property upon which the corporate form is based. The concept of competition is inconsistent with harmony in nature and the interdependence of all things. To control the allocation of resources and services, the role of government expands to replace competition. Finally, Lodge argues that specialization and fragmentation in the scientific areas are being replaced by a need to look at whole systems, not their parts.

At the level of legitimacy, these new values can have important effects. The legitimacy of advertising as a communicative and educational medium, for example, could come under attack for controlling thought and restricting freedom. Whether profit maximization is a goal consistent with these values could be argued. At the strategic level, corporations are already entering or leaving businesses as a result of the effects of these value changes. One firm attempts to divest its steelmaking business, "because the environmental demands are so great that reasonable future profits cannot be attained." At the operating levels, much work in job enlargement, participation, power dispersion, quality circles, and other techniques has been initiated as a means for coming to grips with these changing social values. Ranging from the questions of whether the corporation is a legitimate form to job design, these new values are important and need to be dealt with by managers.

Yankelovich (1977, 63-64) argues that the 1950s was an era in which the social institutions were quite in tune with the desires of society's members: "hard work, economic growth, fertility, population growth, optimism, and accomplishment." Those institutions that were geared to harmonize with the values of the 1950s are less consistent with the values of the 1980s. If institutions do not reflect the values of society of which they are a part, social cohesion and stability are jeopardized. These value changes influence managers of all organizations in their ability to design and operate their institutions. Old solutions may not solve new problems. Universities, hospitals, voluntary organizations, business firms, and other organizations need to adapt to their external environments. The problem of the top managements of these systems is to identify the changes that are truly basic and relevant, whether organizational adaptation is desired, and the mode of adaptation most relevant.

EXTERNAL PRESSURES

Managements that respond willingly to each and every external and internal development lose the confidence of their clients and constituents. External pressures come from many sources, including groups representing splinter opinions. A country club board of directors that accomodates a few powerful members through its rules may alienate a much larger group upon whom the club depends.

Certainly the personal values of members of the dominant organizational coalition can be imposed on the organization through the goals it seeks and the operating modes employed. In top management choices, leading textbooks advise that the values held by the executive coalition be transformed into strategic choices (Christensen, Berg, and Salter 1980; Christensen et al. 1982). Without a consistent matchup of strategy and executive values, it is argued, strategic implementation will be jeopardized by actions contrary to strategy. A difficulty of coordinating dominant coalition values with strategy, however, is the possibility that those values are not in harmony with the dominant values in society as a whole. Guth and Tagiuri (1965) show that businesspeople score higher on economic values than do other social groups. One would expect that result. Similarly, directors of art museums might be expected to have high aesthetic values. The profile of values held by executives is important so far as the reflection of them in the organization they lead is or is not consistent with a system well adapted to their value environment.

COLLECTIVE ACTIONS

Individuals with strong commitments to certain values and their implementation throughout society can usually find other individuals and groups expressing similar sentiments. Religious organizations promulgating moral concepts have existed since early history. The Sierra Club, Nader's Raiders, and NOW are groups formed to pursue the implementation of recently formed concerns. Whether these examples represent mainstream or splinter group thinking is answered in part by the considerable resources that individual contributors have given to support their causes, together with the substantial effects they have had upon corporate operations. The Sierra Club was able to thwart a Disney-proposed California ski resort complex, primarily by arguments that its construction would destroy forever an area of natural beauty and grandeur. Sierra's success in this instance is abetted by the increasing social agreement about valuing naturalness, as noted previously in the discussion of the Yankelovich findings. This external pressure directly influenced the strategy of the Disney organization. Similarly, the anti-nuclear movement has been instrumental in thwarting nuclear-powered utility plants.

Local groups can be quickly and effectively formed to question, review, or oppose proposed highways, power lines, and housing developments. Similarly, such groups have been initiated to bring into question long-tenured practices of organizations. The point of interest to the managers is the recognition that the formation of such groups is probable and that individuals with common interests will seek alterations in organizational performance consistent with the common values of their group. The effects of these external pressures are numerous: the need for managers to spend time to deal with the questions raised by the group; publicity, often unfavorable; frustration in completing new projects; the necessity of changing plans to accommodate pressures; delay and increased costs; nuisance; and diversion of efforts.

External pressure groups may be valuable to the organization by bringing relevant factors to the attention of the managers. At times, however, the interests of pressure groups may be selfish when considered from the viewpoint of the community or society as a whole. In attempting to meet the needs of its customers for electric power, a utility corporation initiated feasibility studies of a new line, identifying three potentially feasible routes. Each of these routes was opposed by the residents who would be most affected by land condemnation or visual interference. When the final routing was announced by the utility corporation, a group of citizens formed, hired a lawyer, and undertook to oppose line construction. They questioned the need for increased power consumption above that served by existing facilities; they questioned the need for increased reliability by a route separate from enlarged existing routes; and they questioned the viability and supposedly lower costs of the particular route selected. The point of the example is the willingness and ability of a scattering of individuals with common values to form and develop an effective external coalition against an organization. The power line dispute was ultimately referred to the state utility commission for resolution.

GOVERNMENTAL PRESSURES

The utility example illustrates the use of a governmental commission to adjudicate disputes among organizations. Although final appeals to such a case may ultimately be decided in the courts, the impact of regulatory, legislative, and administrative governmental actions have substantial impact upon all kinds of organizations in both the private and the public spheres. In theory, a democratic government reflects the values of the society it represents. As social values change, their furtherance through formal and informal nongovernmental groups provides impetus to the new concepts. As the impetus builds, individual legislators and administrators become champions of the ideas, propose legislative and administrative changes, and, if successful, introduce the embodiment of these concepts into regulation or legislation.

Advocacy and incorporating new values into the organizational environment is not a new process. Nor is the complaint by businesspeople and others that government bureaucracies are strangling local discretion or free enterprise by their voluminous regulations and reporting requirements. What is more widespread recently, perhaps, is a more universal dismay from the governed of the perceived crushing magnitude of constraint and reporting in the U.S. system. City mayors decry the preparation costs of the huge justification requirements to apply for federal fund entitlements. Sewage systems, school supports, housing for the elderly, and similar programs have, in response to the desires of the electorate, been legislated and funds made available to local constituencies to satisfy the program requirements. To ensure its will, the legislature creates a commission or assigns the task of administration of the legislation to some existing administrative body. The three Rs—reporting, rules, and regulations—emanating from the administration are one source of complaint of the benefiting agencies. In similar ways, universities, business firms, symphonies, hospitals, and other institutions feel themselves enmeshed in a sea of paperwork and a noose of constraints.

PROFESSIONAL ORGANIZATIONS

The interests of individuals in disciplinary areas of knowledge or in the practicing professions underlie the rationale for the formation of professional and academic societies. The American Medical Association and the American Bar Association are interested in furthering the state of knowledge of their professions. In addition, the associations deal with issues bearing on individual practitioners and the whole profession as practiced throughout their domains. Insurance for malpractice has been an important agenda item for the national and local meetings of the American Medical Association. The influence of the association or local medical societies on the easy availability of medical care has impact upon state insurance commissions as they ponder malpractice rates for insurers.

Professional societies can have considerable impact upon the operations as well as the goals of ongoing organizations. The AMA influences hospital operations, the bar association influences the courts and legal system, and the American Management Association influences how organizations are designed and operated. Although the output of professional organizations may not impose a great many constraints on its members, the institutionalizing of professional practices can have considerable impact upon goal formation and achievement in an organization. If power is not concentrated elsewhere, the opportunity for experts to subvert overall organizational goals to serve instead their professional goals is present. In organizations whose personnel consist of many experts from different disciplines, the dependence of the CEO upon matching organizational activity to the professional inclinations of its most important resources may be substantial. Weakening central goals while strengthening independent professional goals can lead to goal displacement and power dispersion to the extent that unity of effort is unclear, if not dispersed. Professional organizations exemplify external organizations whose power to impose constraints upon other organizations exists and is exercised to some extent. Their more important impact, however, may be their member influences within organizations through introducing professional goals distinct from organizational goals.

EXTERNAL STAKEHOLDERS

In discussing external pressures upon organizations in the preceding paragraphs, the individuals, informal groups, professional associations, and governments have ordinarily no direct singular interest in the affairs of a particular organization. But for any enterprise, a number of distinct locally oriented groups have a direct continuing interest in the goals and operations of that particular system. The board of directors, stockholders, and employee unions are obvious examples of groups indigenous to a particular enterprise. The list of contributors to the fund drive for a hospital, the alumni of a university, and the members of a local political party are similarly directly concerned about the operation of a particular organization. The president of one university reflected the individuals and groups that commanded her attention when she observed that one-third of her time was devoted to operating the internal affairs; one-third to external, professional, and administrative concerns; and one-third to the external groups having direct stakes in the success of the system.

Customers grouped into associations can have substantial beneficial and constraining effects upon a firm. A number of customers of IBM computers have assembled to exchange technical information, problems, and operating successes. Encouragement of IBM to provide certain software and operating systems designs has had a feedback effect to the corporation and its design-redesign functions. Apartment tenant associations have formed to solidify positions vis-à-vis landlords. The power of tenant associations is revealed by their collecting rents and withholding their payment to the landlord until association demands for services are met. The power of the *individual* tenant to withhold his or her rent is extremely limited, since the landlord can evict for nonpayment and refuse whatever service the tenant requests. If by collective action the tenants act in a similar way, however, the landlord's ability to redress his or her grievances in the legal and police system is limited. In a thousand-apartment complex, existing individual families and possessions would encourage the political restraint of the police no matter who is "right" in the dispute. This example illustrates group formation that has the effect of eroding property rights and enhancing entitlement and new morality values noted previously in the outline of the Yankelovich study.

Specific attention to boards of directors and unions as external stakeholders in this section has not been given, but their interests and formation into coalitions with power to impose goal and operating constraints can be just as important as any other stakeholder. The multiple constituencies of an enterprise and the multiple constraints they attempt to impose are not without countervailing influences within the organization that is the target of the external control. It is to the organizational response and internal effects of external pressures that the following section turns.

PINPOINTING SOCIAL CHANGES

If managers fail to keep up with changing social and political values, the appearance of a protest group outside the gates to represent a case against the company will come as an unpleasant surprise. To minimize unwanted effects upon the firm, there is a need for information and analysis of sociopolitical trends, particularly those that could have a serious impact upon the company. An early warning system together with assessment of the importance and direction that changes might have upon various parts of the firm are called for.

Some changes will influence only one part of the company, while other changes will not have any impact. Still others will be pervasive. If the firm is operating internationally, the stability of the political systems and the rates of absorption of change are different in each country, even though some may be similar. Further, with modern communications, issues that arise in one country can be rapidly diffused to other countries. Eli Lilly had such an experience with its arthritis drug, Oraflex. Doctors in Britain attributed deaths there to patients taking the drug, but its sale in the United States continued until it was banned in Britain. Whether this situation represents a communications failure among the divisions of Lilly or differences in judgement, adherence to prior marketing plans irrespective of new information will probably be determined in regulatory or court procedures or both. Union Carbide's Bhopal, India, disaster immediately brought external focus on their West Virginia plant.

Formal identification and tracking of political and social changes, together with the rates of change expected and the potential seriousness that they might have upon the firm during specific periods of time, are the type of information and analyses that are performed by leading companies. These data can be developed by country and by the divisions of the organization that will experience the greatest effect. Some movements will never gain much widespread support and thus have little impact. Others may gain popular support and have legislative and regulatory impact but be unrelated to the activities of the particular firm. It is those issues that directly and importantly impact the particular business that should receive the focus of organizational planning.

The identification, measurement and prediction of social or political changes is a relatively undeveloped art. The science and art of economic forecasting, on the other hand, is well developed and even successful at times. There are numerous pollsters of attitudes and opinions, and a few that regularly report on values held and the changes in them. Over time, such data can be useful in predicting future states and the development of corporate plans to deal appropriately with the issues.

ORGANIZATIONAL RESPONSE TO EXTERNAL DEMANDS

To understand how and why organizations respond to external pressures as they do, it is instructive to sketch a framework of the functioning of systems. Thompson (1967), Galbraith and Kazanjian (1986), and Richards (1982) provide the reader with points of departure, if extended study is desired. The following discussion is based on these and similar works.

The basic premise upon which the rationale for system response is based lies in the predisposition of an organization for stability. An organization finds it efficient to provide stability to the operation of its technical core. With stability, it can design its internal operations in the simplest, most cost-efficient manner. Extraneous activities can be lopped off so that a lean, streamlined system remains to service primary goals. The organization's members devoted to efficiency see danger in environmental changes that disrupt internal operations. The external forces that, if permitted to intervene, would disorganize operations will be resisted.

The organization develops several mechanisms to ameliorate the influence of external variables and their uncertainty upon internal operations. Buffering mechanisms that absorb the uncertainty influences before they affect technological core operations are a primary means. As an example, inventory variations absorb product demand uncertainty so that the productive technology can operate at a steady, efficient rate. Marketing modifies customer requests for special products by price advantages to produce decisions most preferred at the technical core. Special products are discouraged through modular plug-in components to provide customized products with standardized subsystems. A consulting firm specializes in certain standardized (for it) problems. A hospital refers extraordinary cases to others with capabilities that include the treatment of the malady as part of its technical core.

Planning for employment and output levels provides another mechanism to accommodate perceived future uncertain events. Contingent plans provide alternative activity levels that are to be implemented, depending upon the environmental conditions the firm encounters during the planning period considered.

Irrespective of the modes of adaptation, absorption, or rejection of varying environmental influences, it is important to recognize that the system prefers certainty in the environment, rather than uncertainty, and that it undertakes absorption mechanisms to reduce being influenced by the changes occurring in the environment. The human body, similarly, can tolerate only a certain amount of environmental variation. The eye openings adjust to brightness and light glare. Body pores adjust to temperature variations to provide a stable internal temperature to the most important internal systems, especially the brain.

Resistance and Strategic Change

An initial response of the enterprise to external change is resistance or rejection of its validity or applicability to the organization. When it was first suggested that automobile exhaust pollution ought to be regulated, the auto companies countered that air pollution was primarily the result of industrial activity rather than motor vehicles. The industry rejected the contention that air pollution was significantly influenced by exhaust emissions. Considerable delay to ascertain the effects of motor vehicles upon pollution levels ensued, during which the technical core of auto production and distribution remained unaffected by the environmental pressure.

If it is not possible to avoid environmental impact on the technical core, management (or more properly, the dominant coalition) can divest itself of the system being adversely influenced to reinvest the divestiture proceeds into other activities. Strategic changes are drastic surgical relief from change influences. Textron was built through a series of acquisitions, into a large textile firm, integrated from raw material to weaving, dyeing, cutting, and sale of consumer products of the firm. As the viability of this integrated system came into question because of the variabilities of demand and supply at all stages of manufacture and sale, the Textron response was to divest and reinvest in other kinds of businesses, rather than to attempt the long process of developing internal systems necessary to successfully adapt to the multiple uncertainties of the market conditions it faced.

Rhetorical Support and Tactical Diversions

Although recognizing the probabilities of change, an enterprise may wish to delay to provide time to work toward defeat of proposals it sees as deleterious to its functioning. A professor and his departmental colleagues may give lip service to the new educational technologies of programmed instruction, self-study aides, television lectures, and so on, while maintaining tried and true delivery systems in their classrooms. Diversions can be investigated, such as exploring computerized instruction as an alternative, before "throwing out the baby with the bath." Although an organization may long protect its technological core in this manner, new organizations adapting to the changed environmental conditions can emerge to supplant reticent adaptors (Cooper and Schendel 1976).

Environmental Co-optation

Cyert and March (1963) contend that business firms negotiate their competitive environments by industry standards and their common practices through trade associations and other means. To the extent that competitor reactions can be anticipated in this manner, market uncertainties are reduced. Similar approaches can be employed with other external groups. The strip mine operators in Illinois joined the legislature in shaping strip mine regulations and legislation. By cooperating with external coalitions, the deleterious effects upon costs and competitive positions were minimized, while undesirable social effects of strip mining were reduced to more tolerable levels. The success of this approach to reducing environmental uncertainties is revealed in the criticisms launched at regulatory commissions that they were the representatives or advocates of the industry rather than the guardians for consumers of the products of the regulated industry. The Federal Communications Commisssion has been accused of fomenting the growth and profitability of radio and television stations more than improving the quality of programming efforts. The Atomic Energy Commission was charged with promoting the use of atomic power plants while providing insufficient safety in the design and location of plants. The implication is that the regulated industry was able to divert major agency attention to serving the needs of the member enterprises rather than society as a whole. The potential external impact of the regulatory agency upon the industry had been co-opted instead to directions originally unintended.

Compliance

Widespread voluntary compliance with laws is the basis upon which a democratic government is based. The Internal Revenue Service cannot check each individual and corporate income tax return to ensure accuracy and lack of fraud. It must instead depend upon the goodwill of the populace to honestly report income and expenses. Similarly, a municipal sewage authority voluntarily installs a tertiary treatment plant to remove prohibited stream pollutants incapable of removal by primary and secondary treatments. In a period prior to adoption of clean stream laws, a glass manufacturer designed and built a television tube facility whose effluent was "cleaner than the water purchased." The investment in this plant was ten percent higher than it would have been without the water purification equipment. Voluntary compliance with laws or design to avoid undesirable, unintended consequences forms the basis upon which a harmony of organizational actions with environmental pressures is accommodated. Rather than resisting the imposition of constraints from external sources, they are accepted. In voluntarily going beyond the existing pressures, an organization self-imposes constraints that are attended to in much the same manner as any other goal of the organization.

Proaction and Advocacy

The discussion to this point has reflected the predisposition of organizational systems to seek stability and, therefore, to resist externally originated change. A more balanced and accurate picture of adaptation must also incorporate the leadership that many executives provide for enhancing social changes, within both their own organizations and others. The value profiles of managers in private, public, and voluntary organizations do not vary drastically from those of the public as a whole. Certainly, some managers embrace values as "liberal" as those of any other. If such managers are powerful members of the dominant coalition, the imposition of voluntary constraints incorporating these beliefs is more likely. Certainly, there have been a number of executives devoting their energies and organizational support to a variety of worthy causes as well as social movements. The National Alliance of Business has been active in equal opportunity employment practices. Individual executives lend active and, at times, strident advocacy to causes in which they have a strong commitment.

If an organization arrives at a strategy and set of goals consistent with its executive values, it follows that many organizations will be quite consistent in their achievements with the general societal values expressed. One would expect that in some enterprises, there would be leaders in incorporating changing social values into their goals and operations. While anecdotal evidence supports this position, data lending credence to it have not been developed. Considering that the most powerful individuals in an organization are those that have contributed to it for a long time, they are likely to be older and to hold the values socially dominant during their youth. If so, there may be a likelihood of resistance rather than proaction to system changes from environmental variation. Even if executives in dominant positions desire adaptation to external pressure, the inertia of the system through its buffering and uncertainty reduction mechanisms may inhibit how rapidly the adaptation takes place.

SOCIAL RESPONSIBILITY

Closely connected to response to environmental change, particularly social change, is the concept of social responsibility. Business firms are most frequently called upon to exercise a responsive stance to social problems. Nader, however, is adamant toward government as well (Armstrong 1971). The definitions of what constitutes a socially responsible organization vary from one extreme to another. At the conservative end of the spectrum, Milton Friedman (1970) contends that the only responsibility of the business firm is to maximize its profits. If this goal is not pursued singularly, society is said to lose its means of production and distribution, while the prices of goods and services increase to consumers, and capital to produce future goods and services is lost because profits are not high enough to attract investments. Leavitt (1958) echoes the costs of attending to social problems by the corporation, pointing out that executive actions to further a social goal sought by the executive constitute use of stockholder rights in the wealth of the firm for unrelated purposes.

A neoclassical view of social responsibility (Burck 1973; Jacoby 1971) contends that the political system establishes the boundaries within which the economic system operates. If society wishes business firms to provide day-care centers for children of working mothers, the costs of attending to these pressures increase product costs and consumer prices. In addition, if these costs are incurred and social responsibilities are not the same throughout the world, the social costs incurred by affected firms will result in a disadvantage compared with other firms selling in world markets.

A moderate position on corporate social responsibility contends that organizations have the power to negatively influence social well-being (Davis 1975). The unintended dysfunctional consequences of economic behavior include safety problems with products, discrimination in hiring, and pollution. These social costs are the responsibility of their creator, since the firms have the power to create them. The concept equates authority and responsibility as suggested in organizational theory. Under this approach, however, it is difficult to understand why a bank has the social responsibility to provide low-interest loans for college students. The banks have no direct authority over the spiraling costs of higher education nor the relative poverty of prospective students. Yet, equating power with responsibility constitutes the base for much justification of business activity in social responsibility.

Radical views of social responsibility contend that business enterprise should be in tune with the broad spectrum of its environment to such an extent that it recognizes and takes actions to ameliorate social problems. Business citizenship becomes the social savior under this approach. In a variation, Ralph Nader is interpreted as seeing the ideal system as the corporation "tightly controlled from above by the federal government" and "policed at the local level by what would amount to consumer soviets" (Armstrong 1971, 219). It is likely that such tight constrictions upon other institutions (for example, universities, hospitals, regulatory commissions, and so on) would be in order as well.

How to Deal with Social Issues

The preceding scenarios describe different approaches to how business firms respond. There is no right answer to how much a firm should engage in social responsibility. These decisions are choices for the managers to make, recognizing that attending to more responsibility has the effect of adding additional goal(s) or constraint(s) that use system resources. Recognizing that there are so many social causes to which an organization might respond, some observers (for example, Ackerman 1973) recommend that the organization's attention should focus on a limited number of issues, since responding to everything will be ineffectual because of dispersed efforts.

Ackerman recommends that organizations avoid responding to every social request put upon them. In terms of the criteria that might be employed to decide which social responsibilities an organization might respond to, Ackerman suggests that corporations, at least, focus on the following:

1. Issues that are of most *immediate interest* to the firm. Thus, a pharmaceutical company might address health care concerns; a computer firm could support rights of data bank privacy issues; and a department store could deal with beautification and consumer problems.
2. Problems that have high *impact* or *value* to the enterprise. Thus, if water pollution standards are being established, it would behoove a paper company to participate in the debate about the standards because they will likely influence the costs and profitability of the firm.
3. Issues that, given the activities of the enterprise, will *make a difference.* Although it may be fashionable to support some currently popular social cause, the impact that an organization might have upon its success or failure could be minimal. The executives of an enterprise might find support for national drug and alcohol abuse programs to be attractive. Although certainly these are important issues, whether the actions of a single firm can make any difference may be questionable except for their own employees or community.
4. Issues that are of *local relevance.* Since there is likely to be more direct impact upon an organization by the social issues in its operating locale, its focus upon issues of the immediate geographic area helps to ensure that the constraints it deals with externally are those of most immediate importance.

Stages in the Adaptation Process

Given that an environmental social problem exists, the process of incorporating into a multidivisional corporation an effective way of dealing with the issue is described in the research of Robert Ackerman (1973). In the first stage, the chief executive becomes concerned enough about the issue to formulate and issue an up-to-date policy about the matter. Because division heads are charged with the profit and cost responsibility rather than with social responsibility, there is much lip service but little action to implement within the infrastructure at this stage.

At the second stage, the chief executive recognizes the lack of success and appoints a high-level staff officer to oversee company activities on the issue. Because of the staff officer's lack of authority to impose sanctions and because line officers are still rewarded for profit and cost performance, implementation in this stage also suffers. Even so, the staff officer's work is important in defining the issues, gathering the statistics and analyses important to crystallizing the extent of the firm's involvement, and refining the official position.

At the third stage, the social pressures may have become more insistent, to the point that the chief executive feels the need to take a more direct hand in ensuring implementation. Overruling a subordinate or taking away authority of subordinates is a traumatic but dramatic demonstration of the seriousness with which the chief executive views the need for the organization to respond. Although this process may destroy the career of the overruled executive, it provides an example to the rest of the managers of the necessity to conform so that institutionalizing the adaptation can occur. Executives view this process as chaotic. Ackerman (1973) contends, however, that these three stages have a logic that works and is useful. The period of time from the recognition of the desirability of response to institutionalization took from six to eight years in Ackerman's sample. Recognizing these stages exist, however, could allow managers to speed up implementation.

CONCLUDING ANALYSES

The whole field of organizational adaptation to social problems and embracing some form of social responsibility is filled with discord. Advocates of one position or another can constitute harassment to the individual organization. Even dispassionate observers of the concept of social responsibility differ from the views of Friedman (1970), recommending that business firms stick to maximizing profit, to George Steiner, suggesting that a whole new class of problems and decisions will become a normal part of managing in the future (Burck 1973).

An instructive and balanced view of social responsibility is offered in the research of Bowman and Haire (1975). In their analysis to discover the relationship between the degree of social responsibility and business profitability, they discovered an inverted U-shaped curve. Up to a point, increased social responsibility was associated with higher profits, but further increases were associated with lower profit levels (see Figure 5.1). This result implies that firms engaging in widespread undifferentiated social responsibility activity also are the firms with lower profits. It suggests a need for focus upon the particular parts of social responsibility that have the most relevance to the firm. This is consistent with Ackerman's thesis, but the authors do not attribute cause and effect between profitability and social response. Rather, the analysis suggests that some organizations do a good job of monitoring and adapting to their environment, which results in higher profitability and moderate levels of response to social problems. Firms weak in adapting to their market and economic environments are both less profitable and undertake two separate social adaptation modes. They are either unaware of or resist social response, or they attempt to do everything, little differentiating the important from the unimportant. This result also has implications for adaptive modes from resistance to advocacy. The techniques of forecasting and response to competitive or social response are similar. Firms successful at one tend to be successful at the other.

Finally, to those active promotors of social responsibility, it may be dismaying to learn that it takes six to eight years to successfully

Figure 5.1 Profits and Social Responsibility

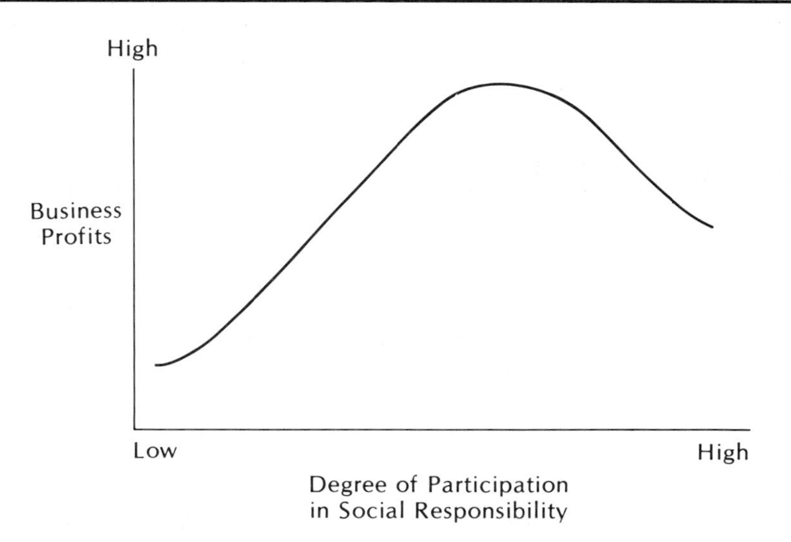

institutionalize a social policy in an organization (Ackerman 1973). In perspective, however, it also takes about eight years before a new product introduction becomes profitable (Biggadike 1976). Large-scale organizations are adapting to their technological, social, and economic environments, to be sure. Whether this process is rapid or slow depends upon one's judgment of eight years. Both social adaptation and product development are, in the author's opinion, dilatory (Chrisman and Carroll 1984).

SUMMARY

Rational goals and processes in an organization can be thwarted by both internal and external coalitions that impose different goals and additional constraints. These must be attended to in much the same way that rationally defined goals are. In terms of external pressures and coalitions, the following can be summarized.

1. Organizations prefer stability to change, since their internal operations are designed to deal with a fixed set of conditions. Change, therefore, is expensive and ordinarily resisted.
2. External pressures, if successful, however, induce adaptation of organizations to these pressures.
3. Major external pressures have their genesis in changes in values held by the populace. A number of major changes in values have recently occurred. These are being reflected in the heightened frequency and intensity of external pressures upon organizations. Organizations have not seen the end of pressures to articulate changing values in organizational goals and operations.
4. An organization that seeks to continue operating on the basis of previously held outmoded values risks its legitimacy and effectiveness in society.
5. Corporate responses to environmental and social pressures include:
   a. outright resistance.
   b. rhetorical support, but no real behavioral or goal changes.
   c. attempting to influence the environment toward goals sought by the organization.
   d. compliance and internal change.
   e. advocacy of social or environmental causes.
6. External social issues have become celebrated causes vis-à-vis the corporation. Models of how corporations should respond to

social issues range from (a) the one extreme expressed by Friedman that a corporation's only social responsibility is to maximize profits to (b) Ralph Nader's position that corporations ought to be tightly controlled at the top by governmental action and from below by consumer monitoring activities.

7. Research shows that organizations that respond well in economic and technological terms to environmental change also respond to social responsibility issues. Such moderately responsible organizations deal with social issues
   a. that are of immediate interest to the firm.
   b. that have a high value or impact upon the system.
   c. upon which the action of the organization can make a difference.
   d. that are of local relevance.
8. By avoiding overresponse to all social issues and yet by dealing with socially imposed constraints in a balanced adaptation, the organization can retain its economically based set of rational goals while remaining in tune with major social changes.

6

Management by Objectives

Establishing goals at the corporate, business, and functional levels as described in Chapter 2 is an important step in providing guidance and motivation to the members of a firm. Yet, these goals may be so general in the eyes of typical managers that they may be frustrated in attempting to translate such distant goals into appropriate behavior at lower levels. Managers at any level cannot set rational goals for the organization they supervise without reference to higher-level and adjacent-level goals. To set objectives in isolation from the rest of the organization can result in suboptimization even if the independently set objectives are met in practice.

What is said to be needed is some formal system of establishing goals from top to bottom in all divisions and functions of the organization. Such a system should relate the goals and their achievement for each manager (and in some systems, extending to individual participants in nonmanagerial positions). A commonly used approach to this issue has been the use of Management by Objectives (MBO) systems.

Most of the examples in this chapter are at the functional level of a business. While the lower levels of an organization may be the ones that most frequently use MBO systems, this is not to imply that MBO cannot or should not be used at any or all levels within an organization. If employed at all, MBO activities should probably be used at all levels.

It should be noted that functional goals may be established at the corporate level in some firms. The functional goals are not subsidiary to those of product divisions or represent operational aspirations far down in the organizational hierarchy. It would be more likely to discover this phenomenon of functional goals at the corporate level of the organization in single-product firms. Yet, Emerson

Electric has been quite successful in cost-cutting efforts subscribed to at the corporate level. Emerson has developed skills in cost reduction in a long history of such efforts. As a consequence, cost reduction goals exist throughout Emerson's organization. The extent of cost reduction differs from product to product or from plant to plant because of the differences in historical performances and future potentials for reducing expenses.

Florida Power Corporation has developed functional goals in seven separate areas: service to customers, financial, human resources, energy management, nuclear operations, fossil operations, and corporate citizenship. These goals are articulated each year. The human resource goals for 1984 are stated as follows:

1. Develop a human resource planning system for implementation in July 1984.
2. Achieve a lost-time accident frequency of not more than .66 accidents per 200,000 hours worked.
3. Train 150 supervisors in "Managing Human Performance" to more effectively link employee performance to rewards and needs for development.
4. Apply formal assessment techniques to managerial selections.
5. Achieve affirmative action goals planned for 1984.

Similar specific functional time-phased objectives are established for each of the other six areas in which goals are set for 1984.

These examples illustrate functional goal setting at the corporate level of organization. MBO systems transform these objectives to relevant goals for individual behavior. There has been considerable attention to the development and use of Management by Objectives programs in recent years. The initial impetus to the concepts of MBO can be traced to the "manager's letter." Drucker (1954) suggested that subordinates each write a letter to their boss periodically to describe their boss's objectives, the subordinate's role in helping achieve them, how their boss would be measured, and what standards of performance constituted acceptable levels of performance. The letter provides a basis of discussion between the superior and subordinate about what is expected of the latter and a basis for review of actual results. MBO has come a long way since that first suggestion. A 1977 conference on MBO listed over fifty different speakers. The manager's letter has grown into a fad, according to some. It has become the consultant's cash cow. MBO is hailed as more than mere performance evaluation; it is a "new system of managing" (Odiorne 1965). In spite of the publicity and faddish atmosphere that ultimately spelled the end of other "savior" systems (for example, zero defects), MBO may survive in some form because it can form a sound basis for extending the goal-planning process from the top down to the level of managerial behavior.

WHAT IS MBO?

1. MBO is a type of planning process between a superior and a subordinate to jointly establish closed-end objectives for the subordinate to achieve within a specific period, usually one year.
2. MBO is also a means for control of subordinate behavior, because closing the loop at the end of the period involves a joint review of the subordinate's actual performance together with judgments about how well that performance measured up to results originally expected at the start of the period. This process motivates subordinates to work toward those goals.
3. MBO is sometimes referred to as a system because often it is used commonly throughout an organization. Standardized forms, review periods, due dates, and reports to some staff organization (such as the office of management development) are employed. Analyses of MBO factors that are useful organization-wide may be prepared.
4. Whether or not the organization as a whole utilizes MBO, any manager can employ the same process with subordinates as a means of linking their achievements to goals of the larger organization.

ASSUMPTIONS IN MBO

For the purposes of this book, MBO represents another link between overall organizational objectives and the behavior of individual managers. It is the type and intensity of the actions that individuals undertake that determine the results that an organization achieves. Throughout, we have been concerned with goal setting and developing strategies to achieve them as means for channeling behavior in goal-oriented directions. MBO does this in a more specific way, because closed-end time-constrained results are established. The goals of a business unit in a multiproduct firm would constitute the basis for initial development of MBO goals for the general manager in charge of that unit. Thus, MBO is to be thought of as a parallel system directly related to other planning efforts in which the manager is involved. MBO goals need to be consistent and coupled directly with other formal planning and control efforts.

A second presumption of MBO systems is that MBO will direct subordinates in the proper directions to higher result levels. By clarifying and establishing achievable goals that are relevant to all the desired aims, the expected results of an MBO system can be met. Yet, there is a long series of steps in the MBO process that can, if done poorly, invalidate this proposition.

A third assumption is that improved results can come from a review and feedback process that compares actual with expected performance. This assumption is much more tenuous, since learning depends upon rapid feedback, not yearly reviews as is typical in the operation of MBO systems. More attention will be given to this assumption in the analysis to follow.

The How and Why of Goals: Vertical Consistency

The relation between goals at one level and those at the next lower level can be revealed by two questions: How? and Why? If at a product divisional level, for example, a 35 percent return on objectives goal has been established as reasonable and challenging, each of the functional goals at the next subordinate level needs to answer the question of how the 35 percent goal is to be achieved (MacCrimmon 1983).

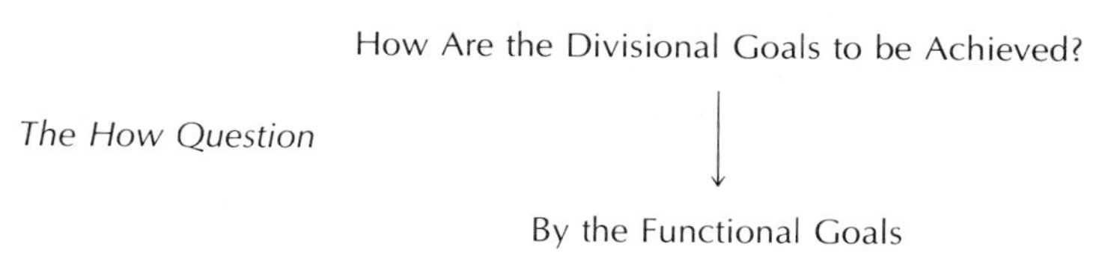

Conversely, if we answer the question of *why* the functional level goals have been established the way they have been, the answer must lie in the nature of the next higher-level divisional 35 percent goal.

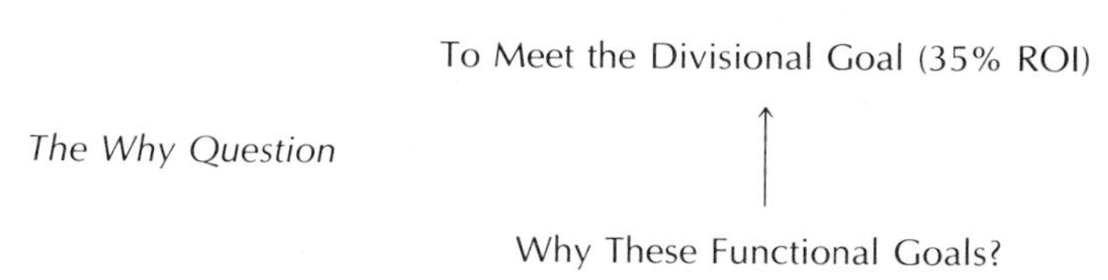

A reasonable exercise to test the reasonableness of goals up and down the hierarchy of objectives is to ask both of these questions at each level. If the system of objectives is to be rational, the logic of how subordinate goals contribute to the next higher-level objectives should be clear. Similarly, the logic of why a particular goal is rational lies in its ability to contribute to the next higher-level goal. The same reasoning that applies to a higher-level goal can then be applied to the next lower-level set of objectives. Thus, the process of asking how and why should start at the top of the organization and proceed down the goal of hierarchy, testing vertical goal consistency.

If the head of a product division in a multiproduct firm has established an overall profit goal in terms of a return on investment objective, this overall goal translates into specific revenue or cost goals for each of her immediate subordinates. The marketing manager for the division, for example, will be expected to establish objectives so that the planned sales will contribute a specified amount of gross margin. To achieve the contribution specified, the marketing manager may well develop specific goals within his responsibility:

- Advertising and promotion budget
- New product/market testing and introduction budget
- Goals about the relative mix of products that need to be sold to accomplish the contribution goal
- Volume and market share objectives needed to achieve planned contribution goals

These goals stem primarily from the requirement by the general manager to achieve a return on investment goal. The marketing manager takes or is assigned a contributed margin goal and breaks that down into subgoals that his group needs to achieve. Note that these same four goals of the marketing manager are all necessary for the advertising director to establish her own goals. The advertising budget represents a constraint on her expenditures. The volume, product mix, and new product goals are informative to the advertising director for what she is expected to achieve with the budget she has. How to achieve these desired results for the marketing manager constitutes the task of establishing the advertising director's goals.

Lateral Consistency

If goals are logically established so that lower goals contribute positively to higher-level goals from top to bottom, the reasonableness of this structure can be questioned if the goals at one level are inconsistent with goals of other divisions at the same level in the organization. To meet an ROI of a division level executive, a production manager may be attempting to minimize extra capital investment (and thus capacity) while the marketing manager is attempting to increase sales above current levels. If current capacity is insufficient to provide product levels high enough to meet marketing's goals, the

Figure 6.1 Consistency in Setting Goals

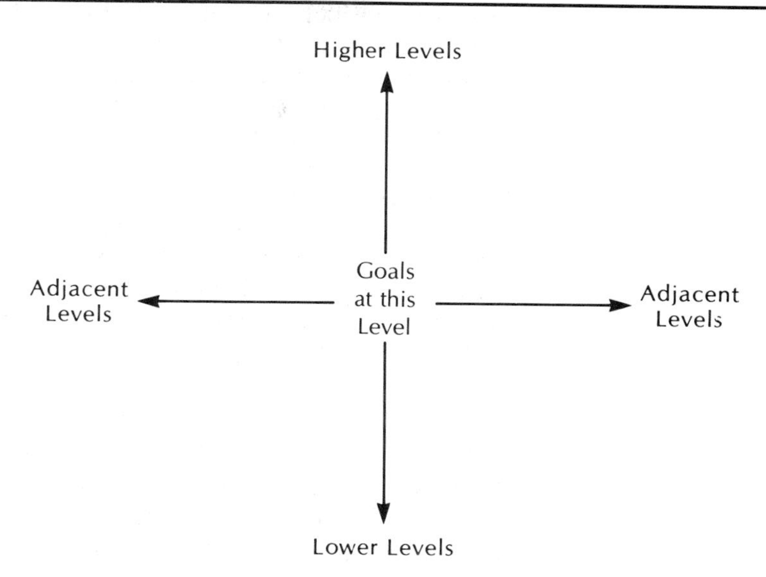

Note: The arrows indicate needs for consistency.

capacity and the sales level goals are inconsistent. While the general manager of the division would likely uncover this inconsistency during planning sessions, it is at lower levels of an organization where many units exist that the dangers of one unit's goals being inconsistent with those of others become more likely. In establishing goals with subordinates, managers may need to constantly question whether the proposed objectives are, in reality, achievable in light of what others are planning in other interrelated parts of the system (see Figure 6.1).

RECURRING GOALS

Some objectives are ever recurring. They are rooted in the ordinary duties of the manager involved. One class of recurring duties is predictable, as the duties stem from a continuous or periodic task assigned to the position. The sales manager plans territories, schedules, regional visits, and so on, as routine activities. The production manager buys raw materials and continuously transforms them into finished products. The dean of engineering schedules a relatively stable array of undergraduate courses in a semester. A production manager of auto assembly may have a goal to achieve

1. an average 500 car per scheduled day rate of output within a 5 percent variance.
2. a quality level so that dealer allowances for field repairs average no more than $25 per car and do not exceed $175 for any car.
3. an average cost per standard car of $4,255.

The production rate goal presumes that no less than 475 cars per day will be produced on any day the plant operates. Less than 475 cars on any day constitutes unfavorable performance. An average of 500 is expected. The measure of the goal of output has, then, both a target and an acceptable variance. But the variance has an absolute level beyond which the manager is not expected to deviate. The measure establishes acceptable and unsatisfactory performance levels. The quality goal is of the same character, but the cost goal is stated merely as a target level. All are stated in the form of closed-end objectives.

For recurring goals of a continuous or known periodic nature, both the predictability of activities and, therefore, the ease of establishing goals can become relatively routine. Another class of activities frequently occurs but is not regular. The manager of an automobile assembly plant may be expected to entertain visiting auto dealers and zone sales managers as they take plant visits. When they will arrive and how many there will be cannot be established at the time the goals are set. The major duties of some managers may not be periodic, but their statistical frequency and level can often be estimated. Disruption of the routine through telephone calls, conferences called, and meetings held is typical for the executive rather than exceptional.

Mintzberg (1973) found the following distribution of work of top executives.

	Hours (%)	Number of Activities (%)	Average Time (min.)
Desk work	22	33	15
Tours	3	5	11
Unscheduled meetings	10	19	12
Scheduled meetings	59	19	68
Telephone calls	6	24	6

Except for scheduled meetings, the brevity and interruptions of activity is perhaps the most revealing aspect of Mintzberg's results. Although desk work and scheduled meetings probably dealt with recurring activities and exceptions to them, the fragmented nature of executive work is most surprising. The idealized image of executives sitting at their desks with their computer terminals, making decisions and giving orders, is not accurate. They appear more as individuals of action rather than as individuals of thought.

The implications to goal setting are several. The manner in which executives carry out their tasks is not necessarily relevant to their goal setting. What counts is what they are able to accomplish. Whether they accomplish goals by telephone or by scheduled meetings is irrelevant. This is not to imply that the ends justify the means. As long as an executive's behavior is within societal limits, the manner of goal achievement, if effective, is a matter of personal style of the manager.

Nonetheless, the random nature of events to which the manager must give attention places goal setting for such activities in a somewhat different light. Salespeople selling specialized equipment need to know the delivery dates that can be promised to customers. Since these dates depend upon the workload already scheduled, the production control department in the plant is likely to best understand and be able to figure out when delivery could reasonably be made. If the production control department takes a long time to respond to delivery requests, the likelihood that the customer will buy from a competitor increases. Fixing delivery dates is a competitive tool for the salesperson. It is reasonable to set goals for response for delivery dates, such as "realistic delivery schedules will be provided forty-eight hours after receipt for 99 percent of requests received, and in no case will response exceed seventy-two hours."

The production control manager does not know when or how many requests will be received. Nonetheless, this activity recurs. The workload is not continuous, periodic, or predictable for any day or week. The goal implies that as requests vary, the intensity of delivery estimation work in the department changes. The task of the manager is to shift personnel to estimating delivery dates as the workload requires. To achieve this goal, the predictable recurring work may have to take a backseat priority until the unpredictable is within control. These kinds of balancing decisions are expected of responsible managers.

To provide complete information for the salesperson selling specialized equipment, a number of other internal departments may also be involved. Goals for response to sales department requests need to be set for these other groups in conjunction with the response time objective of production control. For example, if a pricing group is estimating costs and margins for salespeople's orders and has established a four-day goal of providing a firm price, it makes no sense to require production control to establish a forty-eight-hour deadline. Consistency among the several response goals appears more reasonable. The salesperson cannot make a firm offer of sale until price, delivery and perhaps other order specifications are received.

DEVELOPMENTAL GOALS

Past experience guides MBO cycles for recurring events. Most good managers are not, however, satisfied with the status quo. What they seek are higher levels of performance and behavior. Thus, the director of data processing may plan to replace an existing computer with another. Automation of production scheduling, development of a new sales territory, bringing a radical new product on-line, reorganization of a department, and similar plans constitute activities that are nonrecurring. They are designated as *developmental* for our purposes.

The risks of failure are greater for developmental goals than for recurring goals. Consequently, in the subsequent evaluations of performance, superiors may be more lenient in their judgments about developmental results than they would be for routine goals. Over a longer period, consistent success or failure to meet developmental goals is instructive as to the quality of formulation or implementation skills of the manager. One executive was consistently coming up with innovative insightful approaches to improving his operations and those of his boss. Yet, in most cases, the follow-through was weak. Potentials were not realized, even though the risks were relatively high compared with operating-as-usual objectives. The boss realized that ideally, a manager should be able to achieve both creation and implementation goals. Yet she did not want to lose the creativeness of the manager involved. Consequently, she established a new staff position in which the manager's creativeness could be expanded. She took the implementation out of the manager's responsibility for follow-through by others.

Adapting a known technology for development is less risky and less creative than undertaking something that has not been done before. Today, it is possible to take off-the-shelf equipment and programs to automate the planning and control of labor cost and schedule data in unit production assembly operations. When those systems were first visualized as a means of reducing large clerical costs, however, neither the concepts, the peripheral equipment to record plant activities, the computer technology, nor any experience by others existed. A number of individuals spent ten to fifteen years of their lives developing and installing ever-advanced versions of such systems, until today several available low-cost systems can be used. The risks of failures to the manager were relatively high during early development. Today, they are not routine, but the risks are considerably lower. The creativeness, failures, and searching of early developers are accommodated in existing available systems technologies.

PERSONAL GOALS

While all managers will, under an MBO system, establish a number of objectives for their recurring responsibilities and may undertake developmental activities on a more or less constant basis, it is less probable that most managers will spend a large proportion of their time working toward personal development goals. Executives new to the organization or individuals occupying a position new to them will attend to learning about the new tasks and environment. Perhaps a major portion of trainee time will be directed toward personal development.

The means of accomplishing personal development or training fall into three categories. First are the part-time assignments, whose objective is to provide a needed breadth or skill in carrying out present or proposed positions. Second, a few assignments are made on a full-time basis with the purpose of development for new positions in mind. The third category is education.

Part-Time Assignments

For typical executives or managers, the need to establish personal development goals will emerge from the review of their performance in achieving goals in past periods. A sales manager who had had difficulty in paying sufficient attention to cost objectives may be asked to become a member of the divisional budget committee that reviews revenue and cost plans for all departments. The presumption of the assignment is that the sales manager will—through committee experience—gain knowledge of the whys and wherefores of cost control to apply to his own operation. The personal goal probably should be stated as a learning objective as well as one of meaningful participation on the committee. The tasks of the committee are presumably useful to the management of the division other than the opportunity it might provide for personal development.

Another kind of personal development goal involves assignments outside the firm. Community work or task force positions for governmental commissions provide opportunities for interaction in the wider community, while attending to externally imposed goals or constraints of the organization. Taking part in the activities of professional associations, for example, can provide contacts and insights useful in managing a university, hospital, or business firm.

Full-Time Assignments

The chief executive of a major chemical firm regularly employs several personal assistants selected on the basis of their potential for eventual top-level responsibilities in the organization. Their assignments are temporary, usually lasting two to three years. Then, they are reassigned to positions from which it is reasoned that the perspective achieved from association and assignments performed at top levels will be of benefit. As another example, some firms periodically and regularly rotate managers through a series of positions with the purpose of giving insight into the far-flung operations of the firm. While some job rotation is based upon such a need as determined from MBO evaluations, other rotation programs have developed from the generalized experience that the breadth of perceptions acquired provides upward mobility to the participants.

Both full-time and part-time work assignments for development should be meaningful tasks for the organization. The positions should not just be made up to meet personal development goals of one or more individuals. In positions that are merely make-work, responsible high-potential managers are frustrated. They are not developed.

Formal Education

Educational goals are the third category of personal development activities. Executive and continuing education programs and courses of all types abound. Regular college courses are available. Some focus upon a particular new or complex system such as PERT/Cost or MBO. Organizations planning to adopt such systems utilize educational programs as one means of boning up on new techniques and approaches. Other programs are designed to broaden the conceptions and viewpoints of participants. Short courses such as "Financial Management for the Nonfinancial Executive" are common. Longer programs are designed to broaden the viewpoint of executives from that of a particular functional specialty to the complex multifunctional general management tasks.

In the establishment of personal goals, the closed-end objective ought to be stated in terms of the results that are expected of the subordinate, rather than the activity. Further, it should be well understood between the superior and subordinate why that result agreed upon is a good thing for the person and the organization. Personal goals need to be tied into what the individual is expected to achieve at some later time in the organization.

To put into operation the ideas in the previous paragraph, consider a production manager that has set hard objectives for the organization in the past, has achieved those objectives, and has developed an organization of people and other resources of high quality such that foreseeable future requirements have been taken care of. Remaining as production manager in an already well-oiled and effectively operating group may offer little challenge to the manager, particularly if a capable replacement has been trained to manage in the production manager's absence. Under such conditions, it may be useful to the organization if personal goals are established for her to broaden her managerial outlook beyond production, with the goal in mind that as positions at the level of general manager opened up in the organization, the production manager would become a candidate for the opening.

A personal goal at that point in time could reasonably be established as "to acquire the broad multifunctional and environmental perspectives, knowledge, and skills necessary to lead and manage an organization at a general management level. In particular, the learning ought to include an understanding of establishing goals for an autonomous business unit, dealing with strategic issues for a whole business, and dealing with subordinates in functions with which no direct previous experience has been gained. This learning is to be accomplished in one year."

Note that the personal objective does not interfere with recurring or developmental objectives of the manager, since these have been well taken care of in the past. The personal objective meets the needs of the individual and the organization, and is stated in learning terms rather than as "to take a general management executive program." How to achieve the objective can constitute a learning experience itself. The production manager's superior is, in all likelihood, a general manager himself, so that he could assign the manager as his assistant general manager. There may be other internal alternatives of this nature, but an educational program designed to meet the needs of potential general managers may be the alternative thought to be best. The range of alternatives here is large, so reference to staff experts about the problem is warranted. Consultation with the director of management development about how and where any education to meet the goal could be undertaken would appear to be in order.

Education has become so popular in some arenas that it approaches the popular norm of behavior or even faddishness, rather than a means of achieving a personal development goal on the part of the manager. The writer was surprised to see in the audience of an executive seminar a governmental manager who attended a previous session of the same program. Asked why he was there, the manager replied, "It is my turn to attend." If educational attendance is thought of as a right, a reward, or an intellectual vacation, it is improbable that the experience will be of value to anyone. Unless personal development goals are being sought, the time and expense of attendance are less likely to be of organizational benefit. Although general education is a valuable asset to society, managers question whether their organizations are the vehicles through which this background is to be attained.

GOAL LEVELS

Chapters 1 and 3 addressed issues relating to goal levels, so intensive coverage of them is not repeated here. In an MBO context, the following summary and extension is offered.

1. Hard goals generate higher achievement than do easy ones.
2. Extremely difficult goals are frustrating, in that they appear impossible to achieve.
3. Organizational learning suggests that one period's goal levels should exceed the prior period's.
4. Goal levels tend to settle somewhat higher than past performance. As performance improves, goal levels advance. As performance declines, aspiration level goals also decline.

These are general suggestions that could be summarized as "Set challenging but achievable objectives." When establishing MBO goal levels, however, the specific circumstances surrounding the subordinate's organization should be considered. If more efficient equipment is being installed, the production manager should anticipate improvement in the cost per unit goal. If a project to introduce an existing product into a new region is not to be completed during the interval covered by the goal-setting process, an intermediate level of achievement can be established. If the product is ultimately expected to take 25 percent of the market share in the region, for example, what degree of that penetration will be achieved at the end of the evaluation period?

Past rates of change and their causes can be analyzed for insightfulness in establishing the levels for objectives. A thorough job in such analysis may require substantial data and analysis of it in preparation for the superior-subordinate goal-setting meeting. The president of a firm kept seeking the same rapid sales growth that had been experienced in past periods from her marketing vice-president. At one meeting, the vice-president brought out the vulnerability of the firm to antitrust action because of the firm's market dominance in certain product lines. He questioned further growth in those lines, suggesting that future sales growth should come primarily from new products rather than from greater market penetration with present products. He had tentatively developed his own view of his set of goals by emphasizing the sale of the most profitable products in the existing line. His goal was to increase profit contributions at rates as great as in the past, but the increased profits would come from product mix changes rather than from increased sales volume. This example shows the specific kinds of analysis necessary to match a manager's goals realistically to other plans.

SPECIFIC GOALS

An MBO system depends upon objectives being stated in specific, operationally measurable terms. An objective such as "to increase the learning of our students" is too vague and imprecise. How does one measure what is to be achieved? How does one know that success has been achieved? In corporations, profit goals often dominate the reviews and attention, because profit is regularly measured. It is an accepted concept. It is to the unmeasurable and difficult to measure, however, that attention often needs to be directed.

To "improve morale in the general staff management area" is so imprecise that when reviews of performance are conducted, the superior would be at a loss to know whether progress had been made. Without measures of morale, how is it clear that improvement is a proper goal in the first place? Indicators of performance are necessary else the MBO process flounders. Does the number of grievances filed indicate the presence or absence of good morale? Or does an attitude survey need to be validated to measure it? Personnel turnover? Absenteeism? Combinations of the above?

It is difficult to establish the areas or *content* of goals. It is more difficult to set realistic *levels* for future achievement. Developing valid *measures,* ones that truly indicate the status of a phenomenon, is just as difficult. Because establishing valid goals is not an easy task, it can often be slighted. So far as the MBO system has been established as an integral part of the planning and control systems of an organization, such failures jeopardize overall achievement.

GOAL-SETTING AND REVIEW PROCESS

In previous paragraphs, some insights have been given to the processes of MBO. To avoid repetition, detailed exposition is presented only when new ideas are relevant. The MBO process can be considered as a cycle of a number of stages carried out by a superior and a subordinate.

1. Prepare for goal-setting meeting.
   a. Subordinate
      — describes the objectives of her superior.
      — determines content of her goals: recurring, developmental, and personal.
      — determines measures of goals and levels to be sought.
      — develops a set of action plans to accomplish goals.
      — prepares her statement for the superior.
   b. Superior
      — develops goals he wants subordinate to accomplish during the period being planned.
2. Hold joint goal setting meeting. The purpose is to gain agreement upon expected performance of the subordinate during the next evaluation period. What help is expected or needed is agreed upon as well as achievement. A signed, written agreement seals the commitment of both. Levels of satisfactory performance are prestated and documented.
3. Hold evaluation meeting of results achieved. Using the goals set, an objective review of past performance relative to objectives agreed upon during the prior joint goal-setting meeting takes place. The evaluation meeting has two purposes. First, how well did the individual manager perform? Were there unanticipated or uncontrollable events that changed what should have been achieved? If not, what was actually attained for each previously set goal? Overall, is this good or poor? Since the subordinate often has substantial back-up data about the period's performance, decisions about how well the subordinate has done should await completion of the review meeting. The second purpose of the meeting is to counsel the subordinate about how performance could be enhanced.

The evaluation meeting occurs close to the end of the period during which the objectives previously established in the goal-setting meeting were to be achieved. After a superior and subordinate have reviewed past performance to determine whether the subordinate has performed well or not, how can the meeting's results be used? Merely saying that an individual did poorly (or well) is not enough.

This chapter considers MBO as a parallel approach to planning, operating in conjunction with formal planning, strategy development, and organizational goal setting. MBO focuses on the goals of the manager; other systems focus on organizational goals and plans. Obviously, the two are related as the manager acts for the organization. MBO is also used in other contexts. Just as frequently as MBO is employed as a planning device, it is used as a means for managerial performance planning and review. There are many types of systems for performance evaluation, and MBO can service the same goals as most of them. The following uses of MBO are couched in terms of what any type of performance planning and review system can attain.

ROLES OF PERFORMANCE EVALUATION

There are four primary roles served by formal systems of performance evaluation, of which MBO is one type. Each of these is examined in this section. Performance evaluation consists of a formal review of the subordinate by her superior or others. Peer reviews in hospitals evaluate the individual doctor's diagnosis, tests ordered, and treatment. Performance evaluations by faculty peers in a university often are associated with decisions for granting permanent tenure and promotions in professorial rank. Although variations exist in who reviews whom, in formal organizations, most performance planning and evaluation focuses upon the superior-subordinate relation. It should be noted that considerable emphasis in some systems is placed upon self-evaluation, a bottom-up rather than a top-down approach.

Performance planning can be undertaken to set forth what is to be accomplished in the future, from both the viewpoint of the job and what the individual might undertake to do in a personal way to improve his value to the organization. If a subordinate's lackadaisical attitude is getting a poor reception from others, setting plans to attempt to change his attitude might well be in order. In a coordinated system for performance planning and evaluation, both job and personal plans are established, and then later, performance toward these plans is reviewed and evaluated. Most such systems are simply called performance evaluation or performance reviews, even though the total system also includes planning the expected performance levels for future periods.

Improvement in Present Position

A major objective—perhaps *the* major objective—of performance evaluation systems is to improve job performance by the individual in tasks of the current position in the organization. All organizations exhibit learning such that the overall performance improves over time (Cyert and March 1963). To maintain a competitive position, each enterprise must learn at rates equal to or better than competitors. Although there is performance improvement stemming from mere repetition of decisions and tasks, the rate of improvement can be accelerated if improvement and development efforts are focused upon minimizing weaknesses and emphasizing strengths.

The manager of a large communications group was in charge of worldwide interplant telephone, computer, and telecommunications systems together with the printing and reproduction of voluminous reports. The manager was highly innovative, constantly introducing new and evolving techniques and systems. At the same time, the costs per message and the costs per printed page were erratic and increasing. In a yearly review of personal job performance, it was noted that his subordinate managers and operating personnel never had the time to get acquainted with one system before it was changed or replaced, such that potentially beneficial learning curve effects did not accumulate. The group required systemizing and stabilization to achieve cost reductions. While innovations in processes had been use-

---

Unintended Results from MBO

"I don't know if this MBO program is good for my organization or not. Take Jane over there. She was really excited about it when we started setting goals and reviewing performance because she thought it offered her a chance to know where she was and how she was doing. We started her on an educational program and she did well in it—one of the top students in the year-long management course that our management training group provides. She has been successful in meeting other goals, too.

Now Jane is expecting a promotion and a good raise. She deserves it, too. She has done everything we have asked her, and well. The only trouble is, she isn't the only one. Most of my people have improved their work. It is just a tougher place now to beat other people in the department. Most of them are a lot better managers or technicians than before the program started, yet there are only a few advanced positions that become available for them, and I have to pick the best of the lot. Jane is getting frustrated and may be looking for another job outside the department. I'd hate to lose her."

---

ful, their rates of introduction had been excessive. Upon recognizing this, the manager turned to establishing certainty and a more moderate level of change. His change in behavior resulted in significant performance improvements. This behavior change was not brought about by altering his attitudes, knowledge, skill, or education. Behavior changed and improvement resulted; channeling activity generated the improvement.

Development

Although the previous example focused upon redirecting behavior to improve current performance levels, increasing the output of managers frequently involves their reeducation. When individuals in technical positions of a nonmanagerial nature are first promoted into supervisional and managerial ranks, for example, they often have no prior education of how to manage. Handling a set of accounting books properly involves technical knowledge that might include economics, taxes, insurance, accounting, overhead allocation, pricing, and so forth. If the person handling this task were to be promoted to supervise other accountants, taking care of their personal needs on the job, their motivation, their development, their pay, and interpreting company policy to accounting personnel are examples of the new work content involved. Mere observation, osmosis, and even experience in management are rarely adequate to provide executive knowledge and skills. Development to shore up weak spots and to use the individual's strengths to best advantage in the managerial task constitutes enlightened developmental effort.

> A young engineer was considered to have the potential for a top position in her company because of her stellar performances in a variety of positions. She was limited, however, by her lack of technical knowledge of business. She enrolled in an executive MBA program, allowing her to combine her engineering education and her company experience with business skills for a more well-rounded competency. She stated that the MBA program opened her eyes to facets of the business that had previously been only dim visions. Her superiors, too, recognized that the education had unblocked her limitations, increasing her value to the corporation. She was promoted twice in the period during which she was enrolled in the program.

The developmental needs are uncovered through some sort of performance evaluation system that identifies the manager's strengths and weaknesses, where developmental effort is most critical, and perhaps, how the manager in question can best apply efforts to become better prepared. Development is a type of learning. Teachers do not make anyone learn anything; individuals learn. The teacher provides learning opportunities. Thus, management development is said to be self-development. Although his superior may get a sales manager appointed to a new products committee to broaden his viewpoints about the goals and constraints the firm faces in product innovation, the sales manager can subvert this developmental intent if he merely attends and ignores the content and processes of the committee as they may be useful in better understanding his job. In addition to providing opportunity, motivation toward improvement is also critical. For development purposes, the evaluation process usually focuses upon developing characteristics that are needed on the individual's present job rather than what the individual might need to do to prepare for advanced executive levels. The first requirement for promotion is above-average performance in one's present position. How many people get promoted for doing a bad job?

Learning

The improvement and development purposes of performance evaluation are forms of learning. One learns to do a better job on the current assignment or learns skills useful in a broader context of the organization. Learning theory instructs us that the sooner feedback occurs after the behavior is observed, the more likely it is that the individual will learn from the experience. In the classroom, exams that are returned at the class period immediately after the one in which the exam was taken are more effective in correcting misconceptions about the subject than ones returned a month later. Feedback while the topic is fresh in the learner's mind improves both motivation and knowledge.

In light of learning theory, managers cannot rely upon performance evaluation systems alone to meet improvement and developmental goals. Rather, more frequent timely feedback to critique performance is called for. One type of evaluation identifies only the unusually good or bad incidents of behavior to use in periodic discussions with subordinates. The *critical incident* method of evaluation is the result. As the incidents occur, the superior counsels the subordinate. Yearly or six-month reviews are then *cumulative* judgments about behavior. They do not focus only on recent events, and they are not relied on exclusively for learning.

Promotion and Work Force Planning

The results of performance evaluation systems can be designed to provide data useful in managerial work force planning and in the implementation of such plans through reassignment and promotion of managers. If a system indicates the readiness of an individual to undertake increased responsibilities, direct upward movement in her chain of command is an obvious possibility. Thus, the performance evaluation of the subordinates of a retiring manager provides, at least, information as to whether any of them could be considered candidates for the vacated position. When positions open up in departments somewhat removed from the one in which a potential "comer" is located, some means of matching the open managerial position to the potentially qualified manager is needed. In some organizations, a data file identifying high-potential managers is kept. When a managerial opening occurs, matching the job requirements to the coded qualifications of individuals in the reservoir generates a list of potential candidates. The data bank on high-potential individuals can make past performance evaluations available. More importantly, individuals in the high-potential group would not be there if performance evaluations did not show superior levels of past achievement as well as potential for higher levels of responsibility.

Salary Administration

A final major purpose of performance evaluation systems is to provide the rationale for managerial compensation. The equity among individuals of periodic wage adjustments is frequently based upon judgments concerning an individual's past contributions and future potential. Without a systematic unbiased method of evaluating them, managers will perceive the system as unfair. Criticisms, appeals, resignations, and lowered incentives can stem from unsystematic approaches. Yet, performance evaluations must be individualized to reflect the personal contributions of the manager being evaluated.

Managerial compensation systems frequently possess both a basic portion that establishes minimum salary for a period and an incentive portion. The proportion of variable compensation depends, in sophisticated systems, upon the extent to which the manager achieves the goals of the business unit of which he is a part. If the business is a cash cow, increases in market share and overall volume are *not* reasonable goals to achieve; maximizing cash returns and maintaining market share, however, could be expected. During the same time period, expectations concerning goals to reduce pollution and to provide certain levels of managerial development may also have been established.

Performance evaluation provides a means for the superior to make judgments concerning how well the subordinate has achieved those duties previously established and, as a result, the amount of variable compensation the individual is to receive.

Conflicting Objectives of Performance Evaluation

Attempts to design integrated performance evaluation systems soon face up to the conflict between (1) salary administration and (2) both the improvement and development goals. Salary administration, especially determining and communicating results to subordinates, is evaluative, sometimes critical, and often ego deflating. The atmosphere in judgmental meetings between superior and subordinate to arrive at the subordinate's bonus is not amicable to the counseling atmosphere that one wants to create in evaluation reviews for improvement or development. There are close connections between performance achieved and the need (or lack thereof) for improvement and development. Yet, most consultants and practitioners (Fournies 1974) caution that a meeting to address both goals simultaneously does not work in practice. At the very least, superior-subordinate interviews for salary discussions should be separated from those related to counseling about development and better performance.

Similarly, the goals of evaluating past performance and future potential are conflicting objectives. If both purposes are attempted in a conference between superior and subordinate, the discussion tends to lose sight of the improvement needed in the current tasks confronting the two persons. It is more pleasant to contemplate what the future holds than to get down to basics about what is wrong now (Odiorne 1965).

MBO IN PERSPECTIVE

MBO is a system of performance evaluation to be sure, but it is somewhat more than that. Through the superior-subordinate meetings, a manager learns where she stands. Communication about what is expected and how well she is performing provides an explicit means of guiding subordinates to desired directions.

MBO provides the opportunity to tie in the goals of managers at each level to those at the next higher level. If carried out logically and ideally, the goals at each level would be contributing most directly toward overall organizational objectives. Suboptimization, goal displacement, and satisficing behaviors would tend to be minimized, as goal hierarchy matched organizational hierarchy and both are integrated with top-level goals.

A good MBO process is fair. Bias and distortion are minimized when attention is focused upon output rather than upon personal attributes or behavioral idiosyncrasies. More objective and valid measures of results are possible than with alternate evaluation approaches that rate attitudes, values, and actions of subordinates.

MBO provides a potential method of integrating the physical, financial, and human resource plans of the organization to the goals that an individual is expected to achieve.

Given all these potential benefits of MBO, one would expect widespread applause and enthusiastic endorsement for it. Yet MBO has not lived up to the expectations that many have had for it. Many systems have not worked, and others have delivered reluctantly. Although some successes exist, it is surprising that more do not appear. Analysis of success and failure is instructive. This chapter concludes with summaries of research on the subject.

PITFALLS IN MANAGEMENT BY OBJECTIVES

Lack of Commitment

As we have seen, MBO systems are difficult to operate well. Each executive not only must delve into a complex problem as he works out his goals with his superior, but also must do the same with each of his subordinate managers.

If MBO is not linked with other planning, some rationale for it is lost. Given the perceived high workload in implementing an acceptable program, any lack of rationale tends to destroy executive confidence and commitment to it.

Executive commitment to the value and operation of MBO is the single most important factor involved in its success or failure.

Design

Technical errors in the scheme or operation of an MBO system can have a deadly effect upon its functional success. Instructions to combine salary reviews with those for evaluation and improvement in current performance, for example, would cause major difficulty in operation.

Failures in Preparation

If both subordinate and superior come to a goal-setting meeting or a performance review meeting without substantial support and backup, the likelihood of the meeting achieving its ends is substantially reduced. Similarly, if counsel for improvement is to be relevant to the individual's job, considerable analysis may be required to arrive at an optimal plan for development.

Focus on Personality Rather Than on Achievement

Skilled psychologists may have difficulty in identifying reasons behind an individual's behavior. For managers relatively unskilled in personality analysis, the difficulty is compounded. Even if one is skilled in analysis, the personality traits of good versus bad executives are not clearly established. Therefore, focus on personality analysis is not warranted in performance review sessions.

MBO systems, as described in this section, avoid dealing with personality, but they do deal with the person. In setting goals for personal development, the specific knowledge or skills needed for the person to better perform are addressed as personal goals. Personality, attitudes, and values are avoided; improved abilities are emphasized.

Them Versus Us

Some managers perceive MBO as a good thing for their subordinates but not for themselves. When applied that way, however, subordinates are likely to reply (at least, among themselves) that if the system is so good an idea, why is it not applied consistently throughout all levels of the organization? Higher-level managers can exclude themselves from the process at the risk of lesser commitment by those that must use it. A further loss may be the lack of systematic attention to goals at higher levels. Without overall goals being specified, is it not unlikely to generate reasonably rational goals at lower levels?

SUMMARY

It is perhaps trite to conclude that pitfalls in MBO systems stem from design, operational, or commitment shortcomings. The same might be said of an accounting or wage payment system. Commitment pitfalls are perhaps different for any optional system such as MBO within an organization. Unless the need for a system is externally imposed by law or negotiation, commitment to it may become a problem. MBO, or any other voluntarily developed system for managing, is dependent upon management support from the top to the bottom until it has become institutionalized as part of normal operating practice.

PERFORMANCE EVALUATION IN REVIEW

The reason that performance evaluation and especially Management by Objective systems have been the subject of a chapter in a book on goals is the impetus that they can provide to goal establishment and evaluation in an organization. Setting top-level objectives and attempting to achieve them merely through establishing suborganizational structures with specified duties allows substantial leeway for error and failure. MBO systems and job-factor-oriented performance evaluation systems (if they are not one and the same thing) provide a mechanism for translating overall objectives to the lowest managerial level.

7

Reviewing Adequacy and Achievement of Goals

Setting goals initiates a process of management that follows with (1) establishing the strategies of the organization, (2) using those strategies and goals as a basis of managing the organization from day to day, and finally (3) reviewing performance and the use and validity of the goals themselves.

WHAT TO REVIEW?

In reviewing objectives, there are two issues that concern the managers of the organization. First is the adequacy, relevance, or validity of the goals that have been established and used. Have these goals served the organization well over time, or have they distorted the operation and direction that the firm has undertaken? Is what was originally intended reflected in the actions that supposedly were directed toward achieving the objectives or have unintended directions been pursued?

The second type of question that needs attention is whether the goals that have been set have been achieved. The latter question is confounded if multiple goals have been established, since trade-offs among a set of goals may result in some being achieved extraordinarily well, while others may fail to have achieved the levels originally specified. High achievement of one goal may have been at the expense of another objective. Second, achievement may have been influenced positively or negatively by unanticipated conditions influencing the operations that are driving the measures of performance reflected in the goals.

We can visualize the interactions of adequacy and achievement in the review framework as follows:

Indicated Actions:
Interaction of Achievement and Adequacy

Goals Adequate?		Goals Achieved?	
		Yes	*No*
	Yes	Satisfactory	Work on using goals
	No	Reset goals	Reset goals and work on their use

GOAL ADEQUACY

In the first instance, if objectives are seen to have been adequate and goals are achieved, then an ideal condition exists as far as the period of performance under consideration is concerned. The only factor that might require additional examination is whether the same set of goals is reasonable and adequate for the periods of time to follow. Since conditions can and do change over time, it may be necessary to rethink the content and level of objectives under the newly projected conditions for the future. In both, this rethinking becomes an ongoing activity as the dynamics of environments constantly alter preconceived notions or relations.

Under a second condition, the objectives originally established may have been inadequate, yet their achievement has been satisfactory. This condition is unfortunate because it is difficult to know or to determine how well the organization has performed during the interval that the goals were operational. The Federal Reserve Board is perceived to operate under such conditions. Is the Fed to control the money supply or the federal funds rate? Will its control over the funds rate control, at the same time, the money supply, and thus influence growth and inflation (the important indirectly controlled ends) in the desired directions? Further, the conditions under which the supply of M1 were seen as influential in controlling growth and inflation in the past may have been altered by alternative institutional devices such as money market funds. Thus, although the Fed may have been successful in controlling money supply (M1) or the fund rate, it may not have been successful in controlling inflation or growth of the economy because of these changed institutional arrangements.

Multiple, Achievable, Challenging Goals

The Ford Motor Company has established a goal to make the "best-built cars in America." While the goal may be a lofty and important one for the company during the 1983–84 period, it may not be adequate to company success during a longer time frame. First, quality is not the only criterion important in the purchase of an automobile. Styling, price, mileage, and similar criteria may be of equal or greater importance. Ford has seen the importance of new product updating in its British operations, for example, where a failure to alter its ongoing products has allowed General Motors to challenge Ford's previously dominant position in the European markets.

Second, the *level* of Ford's goal may be inadequate, as well, since the perceived and actual level of quality in Japanese and other imported autos is superior to that of any American car during that period. As an intermediate-term objective, "the best-built American car" may be useful to Ford if it later extends itself beyond this objective to equal or exceed the quality levels of any competitive autos (domestic or foreign). (Chrysler, too, contends that it has the "best-made American automobiles.")

In this Ford example, it should be noted that even though the quality goal may have been achieved (in spite of the Chrysler contention, for sake of argument), both the content of the goal (quality alone) and the level (best-made American) are questioned as to their adequacy for the competitive situation in which the company finds itself in the early and mid-1980s. In fairness, however, this analysis has not examined the full range of the Ford objectives, which encompass far more than just quality. Yet, a goal achieved may not serve an organization well if it fails in furthering long-term interests.

The adequacy of goals focuses on the criteria set forth in Chapter 1, in which the argument for multiple goals or constraints was made. The Ford example of quality (in isolation) would not be acceptable as adequate for the corporation in the long run, as Drucker's eight key goal areas are basically ignored through the formulation of a single goal. Where are the objectives in terms of worker satisfaction and skills? Innovation? Public responsibility or any of the other key areas addressed in a comprehensive statement of objectives?

Measures

In addition, we have the question of what measure should best be employed to gauge the result that we want to achieve. Rappaport (1984) contends that the growth and financial goals that many corporations use, if they state objectives at all, are designed with the wrong measure in mind. He indicates that if the total return to stockholders over time is discounted back to the initial date of stockholder purchase, the total appreciation in price and dividend returns to the stockholders should be positive. This argument depends upon the discount rates that are used to find present values of future returns. In addition, one might argue that comparing present value of future returns must be calculated in real terms rather than in monetary values, whose worth varies with the rates of inflation and deflation over time. Even ignoring the impact of inflation that erodes the purchasing power of returns on investments, Rappaport shows over the ten-year period prior to 1984, the discounted values of the returns for such seemingly well-managed firms as Xerox, Eastman Kodak and Corning Glass have been negative. While each of these firms has had increases in earnings per share during this interval, stockholder returns have not reflected this performance. Percentage increases in earnings per share per year is not sufficient. As a consequence, the measure of financial performance is seen to be inadequate. The stockholders could have invested their resources in government bonds with little risk and higher monetary return.

For example, Disney's dividends have increased at a 34.6 percent per year rate over the last eight years prior to 1985. In addition, their stock has appreciated from approximately $32 per share to $52 after the Steinberg greenmail exercise upon the Disney enterprise. Yet, taking both dividends and stock appreciation into account and discounting these values back, year by year at a 12 percent rate, one obtains a present value of these future returns in 1977 of $23.91. Given the price of Disney stock at $32 in 1977, it does not appear that the company has achieved by the "total returns to the stockholders" measure nearly what could reasonably be expected. To pay $32 for something that is ultimately worth $23.91 is poor investment economics. Yet, the growth in dividends and earnings per share seems to be in the range to which other aggressive firms aspire. If the earnings are not translated into stockholder values, to whom are these achievements of value? To the management of the firm who might use the earnings to acquire other business and increase total sales and earnings? But of what worth are sales increases? To the management, sales increases are typically related to compensation levels. To the stockholders? Perhaps, if the sales increases can be transformed with sufficient margins, to give earnings to give dividends or stock price appreciation.

The Hows and Whys of Goals Revisited

As we indicated in Chapter 6, the goals at any one level can be evaluated in terms of asking why the goal is a relevant one and how it is to be achieved. The "why" question leads us to look at a higher-level goal. Quality is sought because it services customers from whom revenues are sought, and the extra value of the quality given customers exceeds the cost of providing it. Conversely, the "how" question asks, In what manner is this goal to be achieved? Either subgoals or strategies are then examined as to how they contribute to meeting the objectives being examined.

It is at the highest levels of organization that overall corporate goals are established or approved. Yet once established, one may still question why the particular set of goals is viable. Even if we use a most sophisticated measure of corporate performance, say a 15 percent total long-term return to stockholderrs, we may still ask the question, Why this goal? To answer it, we need to extend our thinking beyond the corporate entity to the larger society. Why would society be served by a 15 percent total long-term stockholder return? Part of the answer to this particular question lies in the economic relation of the attraction of capital to such a firm and the allocation, given efficient capital markets, of resources to organizations that society values most in terms of its services and products. Yet, part of the argument may be philosophical in the sense that such an organization, in order to achieve such high objectives, will be able to provide the opportunity for its employees in terms of work satisfaction, achievement, and challenge that other organizations of lesser achievement would be unable to provide. The relation between high achievement and employee returns is not as direct and as certain as the capital attraction argument, to be sure, but it still has a degree of merit. The point to be remembered in this somewhat extended argument is that the top-level objectives of an enterprise must, at some point, be justified in light of larger goals external to the firm itself.

In reviewing the adequacy of corporate objectives, therefore, the top management of the firm must seek to answer whether the goals that it has established for the organization have moved it in the directions that are satisfactory to itself and to its constituencies. At the same time, has this achievement been accomplished with an absence of dysfunctional consequences (e.g., illegal or immoral practices) whether intended or not?

In looking at the question of adequacy of objectives in a retrospective mode, it can also be useful to raise the "how" question: How did the results or lack thereof come about? Was inadequate performance with respect to the objective a result of inadequate planning of strategies and tactics to implement it? Or was the goal set in such a way as to make reasonable strategies improbable of attainment? It will be awhile, if ever, before Chrysler will be able to achieve a long-term 15 percent total return to stockholders over a ten-year period. It may constitute an admirable longer-term objective, but it is outside the current capabilities of most turnaround firms to accomplish such a result. Similarly, firms that are successful on other measures of performance (e.g., X percent increase in earnings per share per year) would need to alter much of their infrastructure, policies, strategies, and the modes of implementation to reach the new objective. Thus, looking at the "how" question involves seeking answers to the adequacy of the goal itself in light of the firm's history and status, as well as evaluating the relevance and professionalism of the planning that went into the achievement.

The experience of the security brokerage firms during 1983 and early 1984 demonstrates the lack of subordinate goals and strategies contributing precisely and positively to the overall objectives of the organization. Brokerage profits were down 61 percent in 1983 from 1982 levels. This condition gave rise to the initiation of specific minimum commission levels for individual brokers selling securities for these firms. While the "normal" brokers' compensation had been based upon a 37 percent portion of overall gross securities commission to the firm, the costs of the average broker to the firm were estimated to be $117,700 per year. Brokers who were selling less than $185,000 per year were not contributing sufficient commissions to cover these costs. As a consequence, Paine Webber and Dean Witter instituted a 25 percent salesperson's take of the commission below $100,000 and $125,000 respectively. Merrill Lynch initiated massive layoffs to reduce costs and overcome losses. In addition, it set forth a requirement that with a few exceptions, brokers were expected to produce $250,000 in gross commissions per year. In all of these cases, it was expected the overall firm profitability would be enhanced while providing compensation to brokers more in line with the performances that they were able to achieve. These subordinate goals were initiated in response to inadequate goals in the past, which were unable to contribute in intended directions. This failing was not noticed in 1982, when the stock market was rapidly ascending and volume sales for the industry exceeded anything experienced prior to that time. The addition of more and more brokers seemed justified in order to garner larger and larger shares of the exploding market. When sales levels declined to more normal levels, the excess staff became evident, as did the low performances of some brokers. These inadequacies, also reflected in the previous goals, or lack thereof, provided the impetus for renewed attention to quotas for performance, a version of goal setting at intermediate levels of the organization to aid in achieving overall profitability goals.

MAKING THE NUMBERS

When managers review the performance of their subordinates, or when they are alternatively being reviewed by their superiors, it is mostly assumed that they will have achieved the performance measures that were established at the beginning of the period under review or that they have good reasons that performance was unable to have been accomplished. There is considerable pressure upon managers to "meet their numbers" under all conditions, whether favorable or whether unanticipated and unfavorable to achieving their goals. It is seen important to achieve, then, no matter what conditions existed during the interval under which operations were being undertaken. Few excuses are tolerated. Results are what count. Advancements, compensation, and careers may be on the line.

To some extent these attitudes, seemingly harsh to some and dysfunctional to others, may be quite rational in light of what the corporation is attempting to achieve. As to the harshness indictment, managers or organizations that allow excuses to be used as explanations for poor performance may well find over time that they consistently get excuses rather than performance. This type of lackadaisical attitude will hardly stand the organization in good stead over a period, because competitors will take advantage of others' acceptance of poor performance to best them in the market. Thus, the choice of being a hard-boiled, no-excuse manager versus a patsy allowing poor performances as acceptable is seen as no contest in favor of the former by a number of managers. The perception that organizations are cold and calculating machines without heart or compassion purveys an erroneous impression, however. One merely needs to ask the question of whether one wants to work in a hard-driving successful atmosphere or an easy-going one, highly susceptible to failure. These two conditions may be painting extremes, however, since high performance and high-morale situations tend to go together. Thus, it is not necessarily harsh to take a no-nonsense approach to performance.

As to the second part of the argument that pressure to perform results in dysfunctional consequences, it is true that unfortunate illegal and immoral results have obtained in pressure-filled situations. In the first instance, if attention is not given equally to achieve all goals and constraints, dysfunctional results tend to be more likely. Usually, managers are expected to achieve their goals within the constraints of morality and legality. When a manager tells her subordinates to get the job done in any way they can, no matter how they do it, she is licensing them to undertake behaviors that would not be condoned by society. If the manager adds, "Don't tell me—I don't want to know how you do it," she probably recognizes that the severity of actions required is so high that devious means are necessary to meet goals. Even worse, she does not want to be a party to the behaviors. Yet as a leader, she is responsible for the actions of her subordinates. She cannot rely upon a defense, if discovered, that she was unaware of what her subordinates were doing.

Are these kinds of dysfunctional acts the result of incessant pressure from superiors to provide better performance? Yes, if the moral integrity of the individual being pressured is subject to bending. Some individuals have few scruples about what they will do and will do whatever is required. Still, others will refuse to deviate from their concepts of right no matter what the situation. Those in between these extremes are subject to deviating from accepted norms if sufficient pressure is applied. It is not the pressure that is at fault, necessarily. It is the character of the manager under pressure that determines behavior.

In the condition in which it is determined that goals are adequate but achievement has been less than planned, the rational task is to identify the causes of underachievement and to rectify the situation for the future. This reexamination would, if rational, start with an examination of the efficacy of the strategies established to achieve the objective or objectives and proceed to an examination of how well the implementation of the strategy has been done. There is little sense in examining implementation of strategy if the cause of goal failure lies in the nature of the strategy itself. Yet at times, the strategy and its implementation are inextricably entwined to such an extent that they cannot easily be separated for analysis. For example, the Continental Illinois Bank, in seeking greater profit and growth goals, undertook one strategy of funding through Penn Square Bank energy loans that supposedly offered high volume and profits to Continental. Yet, this strategy failed to anticipate the oil glut in the early 1980s such that failures of drilling firms wiped out a substantial part of the equity of the bank. Penn Square was closed by regulators. The strategy was only too well implemented as energy loans became a large portion of the bank's portfolio. One does not necessarily question the growth and profitability goals. Neither does one question, to any great extent, the implementation of the strategy of participating in energy loans. It is primarily the question of the validity of the strategy that is raised. (This statement might be modified to an extent in that poor loans may have been made by loan officers seeking to generate volume and incentive compensation for themselves without regard to loan safety for the bank. To the extent that this latter condition obtained, it would illustrate a situation of interaction of the strategy and its implementation that resulted in failure to achieve goals.) If the strategy had not included energy loans, it would have had considerably reduced loan failures. Continental, however, was a conservative bank in few respects (Benton 1984).

The final condition of unsatisfactory achievement and inadequate goals illustrates the situation of a firm that did not know what it should have been doing, and did not do well. The competition in mainframe computers may illustrate this condition. Competitors of the dominant firm, IBM, initially attempted to compete head-to-head with IBM with price-performance arguments dominating their strategies and market share their goals. Yet, with the volume of sales and resultant experience curve cost effects, IBM could, if it wished, meet any price-performance competition in the mainframe markets. The "bunch," as IBM competitors were known, were unable to achieve market share goals by the price-performance type of strategy. It was possible for these second-tier firms to gain a degree of success only when they entered particular markets in which they had some relative expertise and in which IBM had not undertaken to seek dominance. NCR, for example, tended to focus, finally, on the retailing applications, an area in which the company had superior knowledge from the long associations they had built through their cash register business. Other firms made inroads into banking and airline markets.

For IBM's competitors, the original "increase in market share" goal turned out to be inappropriate and one that none were able to fulfill, to any great extent. Turning to a specialty market or unique applications has allowed many of them to survive at least for a while. One commentator, however, contends that IBM is able to do whatever it wishes at the expense of its competitors. This competency on the part of IBM is said to range from peripherals to data communications. If this were a true statement of affairs in the industry—not only for mainframes but also throughout the data industry—the specialist strategies of the second-tier firms may be viable only temporarily until and if IBM decides to compete directly against them and their expertise. The advantages of avoiding head-on collisions with IBM and redirecting efforts to specialized product-markets is clear, however, for the short run, at least. Without these changes, the second-tier computer manufacturers were seeking objectives that appeared to be inadequately attuned to the realities of the competitive environments in which they found themselves. Subsequently, they were unable to achieve those grandiose objectives.

WOOLWORTH REVISITED

Since the materials developed about Woolworth's goals in Chapter 4 were written, over seven months have expired. Although this is a relatively short period of time, it may be useful to reexamine the position of the firm to see whether the goals established by management and then evaluated by the author in Chapter 4 have any relevance to this subsequent performance. The management had established several objectives for the firm in terms of profitability and growth:

	Woolworth Objective (%)	Woolworth Projected 1984 Actual (%)	1984 Industry (%)
Profitability goals:			
Return on equity	16	13.5	12.5
Return on investment	11	11.5	10.0
Growth goals:			
Sales increase, inflation adjusted	5/year	7.8	7.7
Profit rate of growth	10/year	13.4	11.1

Except for the objective of return on equity, Woolworth has met or will meet all of the goals that the new management of the firm set for the company upon taking over. Comparable figures for the industry indicate that Woolworth has been able to achieve at average or slightly above-average rates. Thus, the changes that the management has been able to achieve have been rather dramatic given that their international operations (which constitute 42 percent of sales) were essentially flat in terms of profitability. Analysts (*Value Line* 1983, 1984) had contended that the variety store operations could offer little in the way of further growth or profitability, being saddled with a one hundred year old retailing strategy. But it was the Woolco operation that had drained management attention such that the variety stores had been allowed to deteriorate and their merchandizing to suffer (Smith 1983). By refurbishing the variety stores, individual variety stores were able to garner up to 30 percent increases in sales volumes. Recognizing, however, that the period that we are considering has been a very good one for the retail store industry in general does not detract a great deal from the variety store achievement. The old adage that if you are going to be in a business, you ought to do it well, had not been carried out in the variety stores. The 1983–84 changes brought rather dramatic results, but it may not be possible to sustain their growth rates there, since some of the 1984 gains were of a one-shot nature, probably not recurring.

In addition, during this interval, the firm opened one hundred Kinney Shoe stores, building additional strength in the division that has contributed most to Woolworth profitability. The idea of building strength on strength certainly appears more profitable for Woolworth than building upon the former weakness of the Woolco discount division of the firm.

The other major activity of the top management has been a change in strategy that has brought several acquisitions into the firm. A chain of discount running shoe stores and several children's clothing operations have been acquired. If successful, these will allow future sales and profit growth. The Brannam division eliminated its 1983 losses even while failing to become profitable. Part of this is due to the consolidation of parts of the new acquisitions into the Brannam division.

It should be noted that in originally setting the goals and evaluating them in Chapter 4, the industry rates of profitability and growth were assumed to be similar with what had been achieved in the past. Substantially, the economic recovery in 1983–84 fueled the retail store industry's growth and profits above that which had been experienced during the last ten years. In our evaluation of the goals of the firm, however, we expected that Woolworth would need to achieve at a level substantially above its competition. It has achieved its goals, but it has not bested competition. Woolworth was able, evidently, to grow by riding the crest of the general economy rather than by doing better than competitors. Yet, given the long-term trends that have been evident in the industry come boom or bust, the rates of growth for the industry appear unlikely to be sustained. Thus, Woolworth will need to focus more upon internal decisions rather than relying upon favorable external events to ensure the achievement of their goals over longer periods of time. The economic expansion provided them with a fortunate opportunity to get restarted and turn around the operations of the company.

While we have considered whether the goals that the management set for Woolworth were at a sufficiently high level, given the favorableness of the environment and industry during this interval, we have not examined the question of whether the content of the goals is sufficient or adequate. Following Rappaport (1984), we should consider total returns to the stockholders over time as a measure of financial performances instead of, or in addition to, those of growth in sales and earnings or profitability in terms of return on equity or investment. Following this argument, then, and discounting back ten years from 1984 at a 12 percent rate for the dividends and for the value of Woolworth stock provides a long-term value of $19.46. The only time during the last sixteen years that the stock could have been purchased at $19.46 or below was in 1974. At that time, the low price was preceded, however, by a precipitous decline in the price of the stock from over $50 in early 1971. In the longer run, except for a short period of depressed Woolworth stock prices, then, the firm has been unable to attain a stockholder return consistent with alternatives. The validity of the goal measure, "total long-term return to stockholders," has already been made. It is not the contention of this writing or that of others that achieving a reasonable stock return is an easy proposition for management. Managers will need to redirect their attention to submeasures that will continually maintain margins high enough and in sufficient volume over time consistently to achieve the goal. Many firms, including Woolworth, have been unable to do so.

It may well be that the turnaround at Woolworth will be able to generate the kinds of profitability that will result in the requisite stockholder returns in the future. New acquisitions have been made, supposedly to generate both higher margins and increased volumes. Further, improvements in operations of some of the older units (*Wall Street Journal* 12 August 1983)) have been undertaken to provide higher margins. As these ultimately translate into cash flow, the potential for raising dividends and generating stock appreciation exists. Whether management of Woolworth will move in these directions with sufficient force to provide discounted future returns is a question that will await answering with time. The potential exists.

SUMMARY AND REFLECTION

Most managers see their tasks as meeting the numbers, driving the forces that result in performances previously established and agreed upon. Most organizations establish objectives for growth and profitability, often derived from expectations of brokers and analysts working in the securities industries. Subordinate goals of market share, margins, quality, and so on are derived from and support the overall growth and profitability goals. Yet, growth and profitability may be insufficient in the long run to provide adequate returns to stockholders in such a way that they continue to support the firm with the capital it needs. Thus, it is appropriate that managers look beyond mere growth and profitability objectives to the long-term question of how stockholder wealth has been influenced by the achievements that are being made.

From the viewpoint of society, objectives that may be more self-serving to the managers of the firm than its owners are less useful. Without continuing influxes of capital and the optimal use of it, a drag on economic growth and prosperity results. Thus, society as a whole has a stake in the particular objectives that private firms establish, particularly as these goals fail to reflect values of the society as a whole. The continuing challenge to the managers of corporations over time is to set goals and objectives with which the firm can remain viable, and which at the same time result in returns to the external constituencies. As a first step in this direction, financial goals set to maximize long-term shareholder wealth seem superior to growth and profitability objectives so commonly observed.

References

Ackerman, R. W. "How Companies Respond to Social Demands." *Harvard Business Review* 51 (1973): 88–98.

Armstrong, R. "The Passion that Rules Ralph Nader." *Fortune* 83 (1971): 114.

Banaszewski, J. "Nine Steps to Save Troubled Companies." *Inc.* (February 1981): 43–47.

Benton, L. "Early Warnings: Long Before the Run at Continental Illinois, Bank Hinted of Its Ills." *Wall Street Journal* 12 July 1984.

Biggadike, R. "Entry Strategy and Performance." Ph.D. diss., Harvard University, 1976.

Bower, J. L. *Managing the Resource Allocation Process.* Homewood, Ill.: Irwin, 1972.

Bowman, E. H., and M. Haire. "A Strategic Posture Toward Corporate Social Responsibility." *California Management Review* 18 (1975): 49–58.

Burck, G. "The Hazards of Corporate Responsibility." *Fortune* 87 (1973): 144.

Business Week. "Greyhound: A Big Sell-off Leaves it Built for Better Speed." 25 July 1983, 88–90.

———. "TWA: The Incredible Shrinking Airline." 25 July 1983, 86.

Chandler, A. *The Visible Hand.* Cambridge: Harvard University Press, 1977.

Chrisman, J., and A. Carroll. "Corporate Responsibility—Reconciling Economic and Social Goals." *Sloan Management Review* 25(2) (1984): 59–65.

Christensen, C., K. Andrews, J. Bower, R. Hammermesh, and M. Porter. *Business Policy: Text and Cases.* 5th ed. Homewood, Ill.: Irwin, 1982.

Christensen, C. R., N. A. Berg, and M. S. Salter. *Policy Formulation and Administration.* 8th ed. Homewood, Ill.: Irwin, 1980.

Collins, O., and D. G. Moore. *The Organization Makers.* New York: Meredith, 1970.

Cooper, A. C., and D. Schendel. "Strategic Responses to Technological Threats." *Business Horizons* 19 (1976): 61–69.

Cyert, R. M. and J. G. March. *A Behavioral Theory of the Firm.* Englewood Cliffs, N.J.: Prentice-Hall, 1963.

Davis, K. "Five Propositions for Social Responsibility." *Business Horizons* 18 (1975): 19–23.

Drucker, P. F. *The Practice of Management.* New York: Harper & Brothers, 1954.

Elion, S. "Goals and Constraints." *Journal of Management Studies* 8 (1971): 292–303.

Etzioni, A. *A Comparative Analysis of Complex Organizations.* Rev ed. New York: Free Press, 1975.

Fournies, F. F. "Why Management Appraisal Doesn't Help Develop Managers." *Management Review* 63 (1974): 19–24.

French, J. R. P., and B. Raven. "The Bases of Social Powers." In *Studies in Social Power,* edited by Dorwin Cartwright. Ann Arbor, Mich.: Institute for Social Research, 1959.

Friedman, M. "The Social Responsibility of Business is to Increase Profits." *New York Times Magazine,* 13 September 1970, 32.

Galbraith, J. R., and R. K. Kazanjian. *Strategy Implementation: Structure, Systems, and Process.* 2d ed. St. Paul: West, 1986.

Gibb, C. A. "Leadership." In *Handbook of Social Psychology,* vol. 2., edited by G. Lindsey. Reading, Mass.: Addison-Wesley, 1954.

Granger, C. H. "The Hierarchy of Objectives." *Harvard Business Review* 42 (1964): 63–74.

Guth, W. D., and R. Tagiuri. "Personal Values and Corporate Strategies." *Harvard Business Review* 43 (1965): 122–32.

Hall, F. S. "Organization Goals: The Status of Theory and Research." In *Managerial Accounting: The Behavioral Foundations,* edited by J. L. Livingstone. Columbus, Ohio: Grid, 1975.

Hatten, K., and D. Schendel. "Heterogeneity Within an Industry: Firm Conduct in the U.S. Brewing Industry 1952–1971." Working paper 76–27, Harvard Graduate School of Business Administration, 1976.

Henderson, B. *Perspectives on Experience.* Boston, Mass.: Boston Consulting Group, 1968.

Higginson, M. V. *Management Policies I.* New York: American Management Association, 1956.

Hofer, C. W., and D. Schendel. *Strategy Formulation: Analytical Concepts.* St. Paul: West, 1978.

Jacoby, N. H. "Capitalism and Contemporary Social Problems." *Sloan Management Review* 12 (1971): 33–43.

Karger, D. W., and Z. A. Malik. "Long Range Planning and Organizational Performance." *Long Range Planning* 8 (1975): 60–64.

Kotter, J. P. "Power Dependence and Effective Management." *Harvard Business Review* 55 (1977): 125–36.

Krech, D., and R. S. Crutchfield. *Theory and Problems of Social Psychology.* New York: McGraw-Hill, 1948.

Latham, G., and G. Yukel. "A Review of Research on the Application of Goal Setting in Organizations." *Academy of Management Journal* 18 (1975): 824–45.

Lawrence, P. R., and J. W. Lorsche. *Organization and Environment.* Homewood, Ill.: Irwin, 1969.

Learned, E. P., and A. T. Sproat. *Organization Theory and Policy.* Homewood, Ill.: Irwin, 1966.

Leavitt, T. "The Dangers of Social Responsibility." *Harvard Business Review* 37 (1958): 41–50.

———. "Marketing Myopia." *Harvard Business Review* 38 (1960): 45–56.

Lodge, G. C. "Business and the Changing Society." *Harvard Business Review* 52 (1974): 59–76.

Mace, M. L. *Directors: Myth and Reality.* Boston, Mass.: Division of Research, Harvard Graduate School of Business Administration, 1971.

MacMillan, I. C., and P. E. Jones. *Strategy Formulation: Power and Politics.* 2d ed. St. Paul: West, 1986.

MacCrimmon, K. R. "Essence of Strategy: Ends, Means, and Conditions." *Strategic Management Frontiers* edited by John Grant. JAI Press 1986.

March, J. G., and H. A. Simon. *Organizations.* New York: Wiley, 1958.

Mee, J. F. *Management Thought in a Dynamic Economy.* New York: New York University Press, 1963.

Miles, R., and C. Snow. *Organizational Strategy, Structure and Process.* New York: McGraw-Hill, 1978.

Mintzberg, H. *The Nature of Managerial Work.* New York: Harper & Row, 1973.

———. "Organizational Power and Goals." In *Strategic Management,* edited by D. Schendel and C. Hofer. Boston: Little, Brown, 1979, 64–80.

Odiorne, G. S. *Management by Objectives.* New York: Pitman, 1965.

Pitts, R. A. "Strategies and Structures for Diversification." *Academy of Management Journal* 20 (1977): 197–208.

Porter, M. E. *Competitive Strategy.* New York: Free Press, 1980.

Prescott, J. E. "Competitive Environments, Strategic Types, and Business Performance: An Empirical Analysis." Ph.D. diss., Pennsylvania State University, 1983.

Quinn, J. B. *Strategies for Change.* Homewood, Ill.: Irwin, 1980.

Rappaport, A. "Have We Been Measuring Success With the Wrong Ruler?" *Wall Street Journal,* 25 June 1984, 26.

Richards, M. D. "Providing Perspective to Management Theory." In *Readings in Management,* 6th ed., edited by M. D. Richards. Cincinnati: South-Western, 1982.

Schoeffler, S., R. Buzzell, and D. Heany. "Impact of Strategic Planning on Profit Performance." *Harvard Business Review* 52(2) (March–April 1974).

Simon, H. A. "On the Concept of Organizational Goal." *Administrative Science Quarterly* 9 (1964): 1–22.

———. *The Sciences of the Artificial.* Cambridge: MIT Press, 1969.

Sloan, A. P. *My Years With General Motors.* Garden City, N.Y.: Doubleday, 1964.

Smith, G. "We're Moving! We're Alive!" *Forbes,* 21 November 1983, 66–75.

Thompson, J. D. *Organizations in Action.* New York: McGraw-Hill, 1967.

Urwick, L. F. *Notes on the Theory of Organization.* New York: American Management Association, 1952.

Value Line Investment Survey. New York: Value Line, 1983, 1984.

Wall Street Journal. "Woolworth Net in Ongoing Lines Surges Fivefold." 12 August 1983, 40.

Wildavsky, A. *Speaking Truth to Power.* Boston: Little, Brown, 1979.

Woodward, J. *Industrial Organization: Theory and Practice.* London: Oxford University Press, 1965.

Yankelovich, D."Social Values." In the William Elliot Lectures, *Historical, Legal and Value Changes: Their Impact on Insurance.* University Park, Pa.: College of Business Administration, Pennsylvania State University, 1977.

Index